PAULA CHAFFEE SCARDAMALIA

Tarot for the Fiction Writer

How 78 cards can take you from idea to publication

REDFeather
MIND | BODY | SPIRIT
An Imprint of Schiffer Publishing, Ltd.

Published by Red Feather Mind, Body, Spirit
An imprint of Schiffer Publishing, Ltd.
4880 Lower Valley Road
Atglen, PA 19310
Phone: (610) 593-1777; Fax: (610) 593-2002
E-mail: Info@schifferbooks.com
Web: www.redfeathermbs.com

Designed by Brenda McCallum

Type set in RomanceFatal/NewsGoth/ITC Fenice

ISBN: 978-0-7643-5723-7
Printed in China

For our complete selection of fine books on this and related subjects, please visit our website at www.schifferbooks.com. You may also write for a free catalog.

Schiffer Publishing's titles are available at special discounts for bulk purchases for sales promotions or premiums. Special editions, including personalized covers, corporate imprints, and excerpts, can be created in large quantities for special needs. For more information, contact the publisher.

We are always looking for people to write books on new and related subjects. If you have an idea for a book, please contact us at proposals@schifferbooks.com.

Other Schiffer Books on Related Subjects:

The Tarot Playbook: 78 Novel Ways to Connect with Your Cards, Lynda Cowles, ISBN 978-0-7643-3988-2

The Tarot Game, Jude Alexander, ISBN 978-0-7643-3448-1

This book is dedicated to my father, Paul,
who taught me the love of story; to Rachel Pollack,
who shared with me the magic of the Tarot;
and to Zita Christian, who encouraged my passion for
weaving story and Tarot together.

"This business is so unpredictable,
that the Tarot gives me a compass in unchartered waters."
—Jeffe Kennedy, author

Contents

Acknowledgments

A writer can't shine like the Star without a constellation of other stars to help her.

I first came to the magic of Tarot through my aunt, Indira Aslan, who gave me James Wanless's *Voyager* deck. Though I made friends with many Tarot decks over the ensuing years, it is the magical art of Ciro Marchetti that helped me create my own magic for clients. Thank you to him and to the generous spirit of alchemical Tarot artist Robert M. Place. This book wouldn't exist without them.

I'm grateful for the friendship and Tarot mentoring of Rachel Pollack, who also shares my love of writing. Our writing-critique lunches are magical stardust for my work.

I'm grateful to all the many writers who trusted me to read the cards for their books and writing dreams, especially Win, Andi, Galen, Ginger, Misty, Claire, Vicky, Heather, Cathleen, Alice, Lauren, and Melissa.

Connection with those writers exist because of the well-organized, educational, and supportive writing conferences I've attended. Special thanks to the International Women's Writing Guild and its annual summer conference, and to the New Jersey Romance Writers' Put Your Heart in a Book conference for giving me my first opportunity to present on the topic of Tarot for writing scenes.

I'm grateful to Katherine Sands for encouraging me to write this book. Otherwise, it might still be just an idea.

A big hug and thank you to Eric Ruben for finding a publishing home for the book and making sure the contract worked for me.

Thank you to the team at Schiffer Publishing, especially Christopher R. McClure, interesting conversationalist at Tarot conference banquets, and Dinah Roseberry, patient, helpful editor who made it easier to find my way through the labyrinth of publishing.

Win Day has been an encouraging and supportive accountability writing partner through the months of this process. Regularly talking with her kept me both motivated and connected.

I am a lucky mother of three sons who, though they may not always get my work, always support it. Thank you, Stephen, for tech backup, and to you and Mindy for grandsons Andrew and Ryan, who keep me connected to the imaginal realm of childhood. Thanks, Chris, for tips on promotion and for spreading the word about my Tarot readings to your large network of friends in the LA entertainment industry. Likewise, Jason, many thanks for also getting the word out, and for translating my ideas into music and images.

To my husband, my knight and king of my heart, a million thanks and bunches of hugs, for believing in me and partnering with me every day—and for buying me lots of chocolate truffles.

Introduction

As a fiction writer, experienced or not, writing is a mysterious process. Sit with a group of writers talking about their current works in progress (WIP) and you are apt to hear comments like:

"My characters just took over the story!"

"I was going along full force, and suddenly the story just lost steam."

"I don't get it. I have a strong beginning and a dramatic ending but my middle . . ."

Writing is a wild, unpredictable adventure, a journey into deep and uncharted waters. You set out thinking you know where you are going, only to discover that you've lost your sense of direction and haven't the slightest idea of how to course-correct.

Reading book after book on the craft makes your head spin like a compass that's lost true North.

You don't need a different map. What you need is a compass that works, so that the maps and charts make sense again, and so that when the wind rises, you know how to tack your sails to head in the desired direction.

The Tarot is that compass—one to use when:

- you have the desire to write a book but no idea what story to tell.
- you don't know where to start in order to hook your reader (and the agent and editor).
- you want to explore what happens next in the next scene.
- you want a unique twist in a scene.
- you want to deepen your character's backstory and define their misbelief.
- you need to identify the Black Moment.
- you want to make your setting meaningful.
- and more.

But the Tarot is not just a compass for the journey of a novel, but also for setting the best course for your creative process and career. Use the Tarot to provide insight and guidance on

- fears and other challenges that block you.
- crafting a writing ritual to transition into writing from other activities.
- determining your best time to write.
- identifying personal and mythic themes in your writing and practical aspects such as to self-publish or not, what to look for in an agent or editor, and ideas for marketing and promotion.

The Tarot as compass can keep you on course confidently and creatively, guiding you through gloom of fog and the dark of night.

Before I show you how to use this amazing compass, let's dispel some common myths and fears about the Tarot.

Myth #1
It's a Book of Knowledge from Ancient Egypt.

Uh no, total fiction. Story is obviously at work here. The Tarot originated as a game in the fifteenth-century Italian court, a game that, like a good story or television program, reflected the characters and conflicts of the time and place.

Myth #2
It's evil, a tool of the Devil.

That myth probably arises from sources of religion that believe divination (communication with the divine, seeking knowledge of the future or the unknown by supernatural means) is evil. In fact, as noted in Myth #1, the Tarot originated as a game in fifteenth-century Italy by Italian nobility who were probably Catholic. Also note that two of the cards in the Major Arcana were, at that time, called Pope (Hierophant) and Papess (High Priestess). Yes, there is a Devil card who represents illusion, addiction, excess, and temptation, among other things.

Myth #3
I need to receive a deck from someone else, I need to keep it wrapped in red silk, and other "rules."

For your purpose, there are no Tarot rules. If you decide to treat it as a sacred object, keeping a writing altar and smudging it before you use it, go ahead. Whatever works. For me, the Tarot is a tool. I take care of it, but I use it and sometimes it sits piled on books, stashed on the floor near my chaise, or resides in its pouch with other decks. Although I was given decks, the two I use most now, I bought. I keep them in nice bags but not red silk.

Myth #4
If the Death or Tower card shows up, I am doomed.

Well, your character might be, if that's what your story needs, but you won't. While these two cards suggest challenges in personal readings, in your fiction writing they can provide just the drama and conflict to spice up your story.

Myth #5
It's too complicated and will take too long for me to learn.

If you want to become a professional Tarot reader, that takes time. But to use the Tarot for your writing, know that I've shown writers how to use the Tarot within a sixty- to ninety-minute workshop for several years now. Certainly, the more familiar you are with the deck, the more ideas and answers you'll glean from the cards, but you can use it after reading the first few chapters.

In the 1800s (centuries after its initial creation), two members of the Golden Dawn Society, Alistair Crowley and Arthur Waite, separately explored the Tarot as a tool for alchemical and metaphysical research. Their goal was to formalize the structure of this collection of cards for purposes of ritual and magic. Waite enlisted Pamela Coleman Smith to create the illustrations for his deck. She introduced the images and details for the pip cards (Ace through 10 in the four suits), which up to that time had no illustrations on them other than the appropriate number of the suit's symbol. When the deck, with its illustrations, was finally published by Rider, the Rider-Waite-Smith deck became the standard from which most contemporary decks draw their inspiration and structure.

Why Use the Tarot and Not Any Other Oracle Deck?

While any image of any oracle deck can inspire ideas for your writing, an oracle deck or loose collection of images generally has *no inherent structure*. The cards may have a theme, like fairies or goddesses, but there is no intentional relationship between the cards that tell a story. So if you want to pull more than one card for a story question, then each of the cards from an oracle deck or each image from a collection of images is going be independent of the other, requiring you to work harder to find relationships and the story threads you are looking for.

The Tarot, on the other hand, tells many stories within its structure, the central one being the Fool's Journey of the Major Arcana, which, as you'll see in the following chapters, is also your journey as a writer.

Each card can tell its own story or, in combination with other cards, can tell a variety of stories. The questions you ask, the deck's illustrations, and the placement of the cards and how those elements and others spark your imagination make the Tarot a timeless, endlessly effective writing tool. Especially when you consider the hundreds and hundreds of Tarot decks available to you.

Write fantasy? There are decks with themes of dragons and unicorns and medieval trappings.

Write mystery? Check out decks inspired by Sherlock Holmes.

Romance? Science fiction? Fairy tale? Myth? Steampunk? All of these and more are themes represented in Tarot decks. The possibilities are almost endless. There is a list of some of my preferred decks, as well as online sites from which to purchase your deck in the "Resources for the Journey" section.

How you use this amazing creative tool, this writing compass, is up to you.

Ready to begin your journey?

PREPARING FOR THE JOURNEY

Any journey requires preparation, whether you are going to work, visiting family, or taking a vacation. Even a trip to the market for bread and milk requires preparation because you have to make sure you have money or a credit card, know how to get there, and have a way to get there.

When my husband and I travel, I usually get my suitcase out and start pulling out suitable clothes days before departure. Though my husband laughs at me and waits until the last minute to pack, one thing I've learned from years of travel is that the longer the journey—in distance or in time—the more preparation I need to do.

Isn't this true of writing? These first four chapters are about preparing to write your novel, because lack of preparation can lead to problems, usually midway into the book.

To avoid that, in chapter 1 I'll introduce you to the Tarot; like your toothbrush, the thing to pack for every writing journey. You'll learn Tarot's terms and structure, what a spread is, how to use spreads for your writing, and how to design your own. I'll show you a simple spread to use for your writing using the movie character Indiana Jones.

In chapter 2, you meet the Fool, who encourages you to leap into your story's journey. You'll learn about his journey and how it relates to your writing and story, and have an opportunity to do a simple spread for the Fool.

The Magician and the High Priestess help you prepare for the journey mentally and emotionally in chapter 3. Then, in chapter 4, the Empress and the Emperor will share why emotions and structure are important for your story.

Finally, in chapter 5, you'll learn about the royal members of the Tarot and their qualifications as characters for your book.

At the end of these five chapters, you'll be ready to embark on the writing journey, knowing you are clear about your destination and commitment, and that you have the supplies and people onboard to sustain you through the journey.

Packing Up

Whatever your style, pantser or plotter or something between, pack a Tarot deck for your writing journey. Its compact size won't add much weight or take up much space, yet its value is significant.

But choosing which deck to take can be as challenging as choosing which shoes to pack.

Choosing a Deck

In the last four decades, the number of decks available has increased significantly. In fact, Aeclectic.net boasts that it has more than 1,600 decks listed in their database.

Once you had to find a deck at a metaphysical or New Age shop. Today, a variety of sites specializing in Tarot decks, as well as sites like Amazon, make decks available to anyone who has internet access and mail delivery. Refer to "Resources for the Journey" for listings of favorite decks and online sources.

Access to this plethora of decks is like walking into your favorite bakery or bookstore. Choices, choices.

To make your choice(s), keep in mind that you don't have to journey farther than your computer to get a deck and have it delivered to you.

Choose a deck that appeals to you visually. Writing a novel is an activity whose purpose is to create pictures in the reader's mind and, with those pictures, emotions. Emotions keep the reader turning pages. Choose a deck that helps you easily create mental pictures for yourself so that you can then do the same for your reader. It's like choosing the best brushes and paint colors to paint a landscape or portrait.

Choose a deck that best relates (for you) to the genre, time period, and mood of your story. There is a deck themed to match almost any fiction genre: romance, horror, Gothic, science fiction, steampunk, and so on. Ask yourself what deck your character would pick. Or pick a deck that speaks to your imagination. I use the same two or three decks for almost anything I write because those decks make my imagination and Muse happy.

If you are new to Tarot, choose a deck whose images aren't too complex. After years of working with the Tarot, I love decks with layers of details that aren't always obvious at first glance but that reveal themselves over time. That helps me tell a different story or get a new perspective. But too much detail or too much going on in the cards could create confusion instead of answers for you. Be aware of whether simpler, cleaner images or multilayered, complex ones are your cup of tea. Don't buy a deck you aren't comfortable with because then you are unlikely to use it.

Size isn't everything in a story or a deck. You want a deck that feels comfortable in your hand. If you fall in love with a deck that feels too large, check to see if it has a border that repeats throughout the cards. If so, give yourself permission to cut the borders off. (Don't worry, lightning will not strike you for doing this.) Another option is to choose a deck that comes in a miniature size, like Ciro Marchetti's *Legacy of the Divine Tarot* or the classic Rider-Waite-Smith deck. These are great for smaller hands and for tucking into a purse or tote if you have limited packing space. The disadvantage is that the smaller images could make it a challenge to see details.

Choose a deck that delights. If you like gilding or glitter, lots of color or just a little, you can find a deck with that. Or, you can do it yourself. Search on Google or YouTube for instructions and videos that show you how.

Find a deck that, like your favorite writing software or your favorite pen and notebook, you love to use. Don't feel limited to just one deck, either. One deck and one novel later, you might discover that you have developed a case of the Tarot collecting bug and use a different deck for each new book.

My primary deck, ever since it was published in 2009, is Legacy of the Divine Tarot by Ciro Marchetti. As a lover of fairy tales, myths, and fantasy, Ciro's deck appealed to me with its intense colors and fantastical figures. For that reason, I also love and use his newer deck, *Tarot Grand Luxe*.

I also use Robert Place's Tarot of the Sevenfold Mystery. In contrast to Ciro's deck, Robert's images are more in the style of art nouveau, with lighter, softer colors.

Tarot's Structure

A Tarot deck consists of 78 cards divided into the Major Arcana and Minor Arcana.

The Major Arcana starts with the Fool, number 0, and goes up to the World, number 21.

You can think of these cards as archetypes, what Carl Jung defined as universal patterns or themes such as Death, Strength, Fate, and Justice, and as characters recognizable across cultures, such as Magician, High Priestess, Lovers, and Hermit.

These 22 cards are often called "the Fool's Journey." The Fool begins his journey like a newborn babe, all innocence and naiveté. He travels through the Major Arcana, growing through the levels of development: the conscious, the unconscious, and the superconscious (as suggested by Tarot expert and author Rachel Pollack). By the time the Fool arrives at the World, he is no longer innocent but self-aware and wise. More about him in the next chapter.

The remaining 56 cards in the Tarot deck are the Minor Arcana. Reminiscent of playing cards with four suits and Court Cards, the pip cards of most contemporary decks have scenes on them instead of just the suit symbol. Unlike playing cards, instead of the three royals (Jack, Queen, King), there are four royals, usually called Pages, Knights, Queens, and Kings. Some decks name them differently, but they still represent that energy or essence.

Each suit in the Tarot represents an element, a direction, and an aspect of being human.

Swords	Air	East	Mind
Wands	Fire	South	Spirit
Cups	Water	West	Heart
Coins	Earth	North	Body

The four suits/elements and their influences are

Swords (Air)—associated with mind, thoughts, attitudes, beliefs, communication (writing), teaching, inspiration, creativity.

Wands (Fire)—associated with spirit, creativity, career, work, inner drive, vision, creativity.

Cups (Water)—associated with the heart, emotions, love, relationships, dreams, intuition, longing, creativity.

Coins or Pentacles (Earth)—associated with the material world, home, health, wealth, the five senses, creativity.

Some decks reverse Swords and Wands. If that bothers you, then be sure you've checked the deck out before you buy it. Also, depending on the theme or genre of the deck, Coins may be called Pentacles or Disks, Cups may be called Vessels or Chalices, and Wands may be called Staffs, Sticks, or even Spears. The thing to keep in mind is the division into four and their relationship to the four elements and the four aspects of being human.

Each of the four suits lists creativity as one of their qualities. The reason for this is that creativity, including writing, which might seem to be solely a mind activity, involves all four aspects of being human. Heart, mind, body, and soul all work together and separately to make your story a reality. All four aspects are necessary to create.

Numbers

One of the easiest ways to work with the Minor Arcana if you are new to the Tarot is to combine the elemental energy (Air, Fire, Water, Earth) of the deck with the energy of the number on the card:

1: Beginnings, initiations, seed, spark or idea, singularity

2: Partnering, dialogue, connection, communication, choice or decision

3: Expansion, growth, early fulfillment, creativity

4: Foundations, consolidation, structure, commitment

5: Change, loss, struggle, competition

6: Rewards, new confidence, balance in relationships (or lack thereof)

7: Unexpected challenges, upheaval, risk-taking, focus, contemplation

8: Maturity, consolidation, peak of ability, movement toward goals

9: Endings, completion, intensity, preparing for the next cycle

10: Abundance (or overabundance), transition, turning of the cycle, tipping point

Royals

After the pip cards (1–10), you have the Court Cards. Again, you can combine the suit with the role of the royal on the card for ideas for character in your story or a person in your writing life. In chapter 5, you'll learn about each royal of each suit in more detail. For now, keep these general ideas in mind:

Page: In days of yore, when people lived and worked in castles, the pages were youthful figures who had vitality and an eagerness to please and do. The page served as messenger for a nobleman or knight. The negative or challenging aspect might be too much innocence, enthusiasm, or inexperience.

Knight: The knight, older and more experienced than the page, is trained in weaponry and battle in order to serve and protect the realm. He's the gallant champion, idealistic and responsible, but sometimes too eager to do battle, to run to the rescue whether it is necessary or not.

Queen: The mature woman who appreciates life and inspires others to action rather than commanding it. She nourishes and nurtures and pays attention to details. She might be too nurturing when she should be kicking the chick out of the nest.

King: The man of power who, it is hoped, has wisdom and responsibility, who knows how to rule for the benefit of all, and how to delegate to make things happen. If he lacks an emotional balance, he can be power hungry, domineering, and too focused on the big picture to see important details.

As you become familiar with the scenes on the cards, taking into consideration the actions of the figures and how they relate to each other, along with the objects, the colors, and the mood of the cards, you'll easily discover ideas for story—especially when you use them in a spread.

What Is a Spread?

A spread is a pattern of chosen positions for pulling and laying out cards. Each position in the pattern is a place holder for a particular meaning or significance.

A spread consists of one card, several cards, or the whole deck. When you first do readings or design spreads for your work, use one to five cards. Once you are comfortable with the process, add more cards. A variety of spreads for the writing journey and your story are in this book, but if you want to create your own, first clarify and define what you want to know. As in plotting and story development, questions are key.

For example, if you write yourself into a corner, the most obvious and simple question to ask is "How do I get my hero/ine out of this situation?" One card might provide an answer, or you could pull several cards for more detail and possibilities. If you don't like what cards show up or don't understand what they are telling you, pull more cards until something clicks.

I can't reiterate enough that the Tarot is a tool for your writing. Use it in whatever way achieves the results you want. Neither I nor any other Tarotist will be looking over your shoulder to see if you are doing it "right." There is no right; there is only do. Wait, I mangled the quote. Anyway, you get the picture.

And just to be sure you do, here's a common three-card spread you can use for any character—past, present, and future.

Indiana Jones Past-Present-Future Spread

Because I am going to talk about him in the next chapter on the Fool, let's do a spread for Indiana Jones in *The Last Crusade*. The question would be "What do I need to know (as the writer) about Indiana's past, present, and future for this screenplay?"

I shuffled Ciro Marchetti's *Retrospective Tarot* and pulled these three cards in order of past, present, and future.

PAST—
Strength, *Retrospective Tarot* by, and courtesy of, Ciro Marchetti.

PRESENT—
8 of Cups, *Retrospective Tarot* by, and courtesy of, Ciro Marchetti.

FUTURE—
Judgement, *Retrospective Tarot* by, and courtesy of, Ciro Marchetti.

Note that two out of three cards are Major Arcana cards, so, as the movie opens, Indiana is dealing with mythic themes in both his past and his future.

In the first card, Strength, we are reminded that though Indiana may seem like a mild-mannered professor of archeology, he is, in fact, an adventurous archeological treasure hunter, traveling to places that are wild and untamed in his search. From previous films, you know that he has plenty of courage and confidence when it comes to angry natives, scheming Nazis, and other nefarious villains. He conquers the wild places not with brute strength but more often trickery and charm that arise from the inner confidence he has about his abilities and knowledge.

The second card, his present, is the 8 of Cups. Cups is the element of Water, the realm of the heart. Here is a man who finds his current passions weighing him down. Eight is a number of movement toward goals. The man's back is to us as if he moves away, but below the surface of the water, his tentacles cling to the eight cups. In the present, Indy is offered a new dream to chase if he can let go of some other relationships and attachments. It is no coincidence that the new chase for Indy is to find the cup of all cups, the Holy Grail.

Finally, the card in the position of Indiana's future, Judgment. In most cases, Judgment is not about being judged but about rebirth, a calling to new life. Indy's father, Henry, lies mortally wounded and dying. After Indy risks his own death (more on that in the next chapter) to get the Holy Grail and its healing water to his dying father, they emerge from the temple as from the womb, reborn in their relationship to each other.

Use this simple spread for your characters before you begin to write and as you think about your character's backstory.

Taking the Risk, Making the Leap

Have you flown anywhere recently?

It's more of an adventure—and not a good one, with cancellations, delays, overbooking, and lost luggage. Even with all the technological advances and the institution of safety regulations, traveling is a risk, whether by plane, train, or car, on two feet, or riding a bicycle.

Fool

And so, the Major Arcana starts with the risk taker, the Fool, number 0. Just like what you have at the beginning of writing a new story—zero.

Risk

Zero words, the proverbial blank slate. Maybe you have a glimmer of an idea or a character who's taken up residence in your mind, but at the beginning of your writing journey, the possibilities—and the hazards—are endless.

That zero also represents a state of innocence. The Fool takes a risk because he really doesn't have the experience to know better.

The Fool,
Legacy of the Divine Tarot by Ciro Marchetti.
Courtesy of Llewellyn Worldwide, Ltd.

On some cards, the Fool appears to be stepping off a high cliff—or off the hourglass—not looking where he is going. Because if you could see the future, you might not take that risk. Risks like asking someone to marry you, or getting pregnant, or taking a new job. Or writing a book.

Let's go back to Indiana Jones and the Last Crusade. Near the end of the film, Indy's father, Henry, is shot in order to force Indy to move through a series of booby traps, capture the Holy Grail, and bring it back to the waiting bad guy. The only way to keep his father from dying is to bring him water in that cup.

In my favorite scene, Indy successfully makes it through the traps by following the small drawings and notes in his father's diary, until he arrives and almost falls into the abyss that separates him from the temple where the Grail Knight guards the cup. (In addition to Indy's Fool, there is now a Knight of Cups!)

Indy checks his father's diary showing the sketch of a bridge or walkway over the abyss. He can't see it, but all of his father's previous directions and clues proved true. Scooping up a handful of dirt, Indy throws it out and the falling dust reveals the bridge.

As the dirt slips away and the bridge seems to disappear, his father's friend yells to him, "Hurry, Indy." He has no choice but to step out in trust and faith in his father. Closing his eyes, he takes the first step braced for the fall.

In that moment, Indy is the perfect example of the Fool.

Instinct

The Fool sets out, maybe with a destination in mind. Maybe not. His belongings are tied in a bundle to the stick carried over his shoulder. With him is an animal companion, usually a dog, representing instinct and pushing the Fool to act.

With that first idea for a book, you start writing, acting on instinct. If you stopped to think about the work ahead to write thousands of words, you might never start.

Instead, a writer gets caught up in the emotion, in the excitement of the new story. Responding to instinct, you are off into what if and why, excited about the journey ahead.

If you bring the energy of the Fool into your writing, that mindset of innocence and optimism, of being a clean slate no matter how many books you've written before, no matter how many successes—or failures—you've experienced, then you start your journey off with hope.

Even when stepping off into an abyss.

Being the Fool is not just about risk and instinct. It's about a willingness to look foolish for our writing, regardless of what others think and say. Yes, your first venture into writing a book, without a contract or payment, may look foolish to family and friends, but would you really rather not take the journey?

Sometimes being a Fool is smart.

Even when stepping off into an abyss.

Here and at the end of chapters 3, 4, and 6–14 are questions for you and your writing journey and for your characters. Use these questions with each new story as journal questions or individually or together as the basis for a spread. Be willing to feel foolish as you start working with the cards. Trust your instincts.

You as the Fool

1. How many times have you started a manuscript, written the first few pages or chapters, and then put it away? Why?

2. What do you need to change about your beliefs about your writing in order to leap into the book you want to write with a sense of "Whee-e-e-e!" instead of "Well, maybe . . ."?

3. What did you do as a child that felt both exciting and scary? Can you recapture that feeling for this book? Can you recapture that mindset of anything is possible?

To create a spread for any of these questions, pull cards for different aspects of the question. For example, for question number 2, you could do a one-card, three-card, or five-card spread.

The one-card would answer the question in general.

The three-card would look at what you believe about your writing, what you believe about yourself, and what you can do to change those beliefs.

The five-card spread would include a card for you, the three cards above, and the final card to represent the outcome—the effect on you and your writing if you made the changes.

Your Character as the Fool

Every hero or heroine at the beginning of a story is the Fool. They start a journey that brings new experiences and understandings that change and transform them. They must risk life, love, loss, and more.

Sometimes they are forced into taking the leap, and other times they choose to leap.

Besides the hero, other characters as the Fool could be children or anyone innocent, happy-go-lucky, or someone always on the move. Or think of the gambler who loves the adrenaline rush of risk, or the woman who keeps falling in love just for the excitement of it.

In fiction, film, or television, the Fool stepping off the cliff is Wile E. Coyote, Alice pursuing the White Rabbit down the rabbit hole, Luke Skywalker leaving his home planet of Tatooine, or Dorothy starting down the Yellow Brick Road.

The Fool's Questions for your Characters

1. What initial leap, risk, or entry into a new world does your hero or heroine take at the beginning of your story? Is it big enough to catapult your character into the story?

2. At the beginning, what does your character not see or refuse to see? This could also be a misbelief as Lisa Cron talks about in her book Story Genius.

3. What does your character have to fear about this leap?

4. What instinct pushes your character to make the leap (such as curiosity, compassion, competition, etc.)?

5. What is your character's goal when they make the leap? Will it change? How?

6. Is there a companion (doesn't have to be four legged), like the Fool's dog, that encourages the leap?

For a Fool spread, use one of the questions or intentionally pull out the Fool card in your deck. Then shuffle the deck and lay out four cards in a line after it. The first card after the Fool represents the leap, the next card is the fear, the third card represents the change, and the final card represents the result or outcome. What shows up? Remember, this is play. If you pull five cards and nothing sparks, reshuffle and pull more.

Before you refer back to the numbers and other information in the last chapter, look at the cards and ask:

- What direction are the figures in the cards facing—to the right (future or to the next card), to the left (past or to the last card), or to the front (present), suggesting how characters or events relate. Think of how the man had his back to you in the reading for Indy. He was moving away from you, from whatever was behind him.
- Where do your eyes go first on each card? That may be the element or action that answers your question. Remember the lion on the Strength card for Indy?
- What is the mood or emotion of the card? On the Judgment card there is a feeling of celebration or excitement.

You don't need to know the traditional meanings of the cards for them to help you tell your story. Be a Fool for the Tarot.

Now that you've allowed yourself to play and feel a little foolish, are you ready to meet the Magician and the High Priestess?

Then, as Van Halen would say, "Go ahead and jump."

Packing Up
Your Outer and Inner
Resources

A new journey is never just a matter of buying a ticket, clearing your schedule, or packing up your hobo bag, especially if it is a journey over untraveled waters. Travel requires planning and preparation both inwardly and outwardly.

The Magician,
Tarot of the Sevenfold Mystery
by, and courtesy of, Robert M. Place.

The High Priestess,
Tarot of the Sevenfold Mystery
by, and courtesy of, Robert M. Place.

As the Fool ventures forth, as you write the first words of your story, as your hero or heroine takes those first steps into their new normal, the first encounters along the journey are the Magician and the High Priestess.

Magician

In the earliest versions of Tarot decks, like the *Marseilles*, the Magician appears to be more scam artist or mountebank than performer. He stands at a table with a variety of objects before him, not to call down the energy of creation, but to provide easy entertainment in the form of that still-popular now-you-see-it-now-you-don't con, the shell game. In it, the player, a.k.a. "the mark," bets that he can pick under which cup or shell of three the pea, or some other small object, is to be found.

Focus

As con artist, for the Magician to win more than he loses, he must control the focus of his audience or players. As he shuffles those shells around, he wants the player to lose focus, to lose track of which shell hides the pea, or to be so focused on the shells that he doesn't see the Magician actually remove the pea. The Magician can't break his focus or he'll break the focus of the player.

For what is traditionally thought of as a magician—someone who performs ritual or natural magic—control of the focus is still critical. Even in today's modern concept of magic (i.e., illusions and tricks), losing focus means losing audience and money, and sometimes, as in the case of Houdini's Chinese Water Torture Tank, life.

In the Magician card from the Rider-Waite-Smith deck or other decks, the Magician stands with the finger of one hand (or a wand in that hand) pointing heavenward and the finger of the other hand pointing to the Earth. In this position, he is an open channel for the movement of energy from the plane of thought or idea to the plane of manifestation in physical form.

The Magician uses a one-pointed focus to make magic happen, which is why you'll often see magicians with magic wands—because it focuses the magician and the energy, just as your pen or your fingers on the keyboard focus your creative magic as you channel the inspiration of your Muse.

Focus requires attention.

Think about some of your favorite magicians, such as Gandalf or Dumbledore or Merlin, each with their wand or staff. In ritual, the wand is used to focus attention and move energy. Contemporary magicians don't use a wand. Instead, they will point a finger—just like the Tarot's Magician—or their whole arm and hand will wave or gesture to where your attention should be.

Writers do the same thing at the beginning of a new book, using certain details of setting and the introduction of certain characters to grab and focus the attention of the reader. This focus is usually called the hook, and without that strong focus or hook, the writer can lose the reader, including an agent or editor. Once captured, the focus and attention of the reader has to be maintained to keep the reader turning pages.

The hero/ine of a story must also maintain focus on what they want or desire. If focus on the desire isn't strong enough to prevail in spite of obstacles, then there is no conflict.

Confidence

The second quality the Magician role-models for the writer is confidence. Confidence in his ability to maintain his focus and his audience's. Confidence in his ability to channel energy from idea to manifestation.

Did you ever see David Copperfield perform? It takes a huge amount of confidence to carry off the illusion of making an Orient Express train car or the Statue of Liberty disappear. Just as it took a huge amount of confidence and courage for Gandalf to confront the Balrog in The Lord of the Rings.

As a writer, you need confidence as you set out on the journey of your story. Without it, you'll fail to keep writing or keep the focus and attention of the reader on the story.

Your hero's or heroine's journey either starts with confidence that is later shaken or discovers their confidence and builds it throughout the story, as with many coming-of-age stories like Harry Potter.

Focus and confidence, two of the positive aspects of the Magician. Other positive aspects include creativity, the ability to manifest idea in physical form, and the power to be persuasive and take action.

When his power is distorted or blocked, he's an illusionist without substance, a trickster. He can be manipulative, showy, and corrupt. In his negative aspect, it's all about the surface, what he can persuade you to believe you are seeing or experiencing.

But when the Magician is clear about his power and purpose? That's when the real magic happens, when transformation occurs.

The Magician's Questions for You

1. Are you an open channel for creative ideas or do you try to control the process and flow of the story?

2. What tools do you need to support your writing? Physical, such as space, notebooks, pictures, etc.; mental, such as confidence in your ability to tell your

story; emotional, such as a sense of power, excitement, or desire; spiritual, such as a sense of higher purpose?

3. Where is your focus and attention today? Is it on your writing? What helps you focus on it?

4. What can you do to maintain your confidence on your journey? Do you need inspiring posters, music, or supportive friends?

Your Character as Magician

In fiction, the Magician is Gandalf or Dumbledore, able to discern energies and patterns that others miss, and then weave them together into a desired result. Or Dr. Frankenstein, thinking to control the power of life and death. Or Cinderella's fairy godmother with her star-tipped wand, helping to transform Cinderella's life and bring her that happily ever after.

Often the Magician is a secondary character, someone who aids the hero or heroine. Conversely, like the Wicked Witch of the West, the Magician is there to plot and plan destruction. Or he's the mountebank, the charlatan, using his skills of deception to cheat people out of their money or goods.

As powerful as the Magician may be, he or she often faces a test that either transforms them or kills them. If transformed, they are gifted with new powers and abilities, deeper insights.

The Magician's Questions for Your Character

1. Who has the power of transformation? The hero or heroine, or a supporting character?

2. Is your Magician an artist, an entertainer, a scientist, a businessman, or a mystic?

3. Is his or her magic authentic, or is it a trick, used to manipulate or cheat others?

4. What tools does he or she use—physical or otherwise?

5. How is he or she directing—or misdirecting—attention in order to achieve the desired goal?

6. If your Magician is the villain in the story, how do his skills and personality challenge the hero or heroine?

As a suggested spread for the gesture of the Magician, pull three cards—one to represent focus (for you, your story, or a character), one to represent where the attention (of you, the reader, or another character) needs to be, and a third card between the two to represent how the energy is being moved from focus or idea to attention and manifestation. As suggested in the last chapter, look at the relationship of the cards to each other. Note where your eyes go first, the mood or emotion you pick up from the cards. Then look at the significance of the numbers, the elements, and the colors, even the gestures of the figures.

High Priestess

The Magician starts you on your way, but the High Priestess tests you to be sure you are ready for the journey.

When the Viscontis commissioned the first Tarot deck, the trump or Major Arcana card that followed the Magician was known as La Papessa, reminiscent of a female pope, Manfreda Visconti. Later, in the eighteenth century, when the Europeans had a fascination with all things Egyptian and it was thought that the Tarot arose out of the religion of Isis, the name of the card was changed to the High Priestess.

For your writing and your novel, here are two ways that the High Priestess moves you further on your way, into the deeper realms of your story.

Threshold Guardian

In many Tarot decks, the High Priestess is positioned at a threshold or doorway, often with two pillars to either side of her, like a threshold guardian. She is the first threshold guardian you encounter in writing your story, and that your character(s) encounter.

Christopher Vogler, in his popular book *The Writer's Journey*, says that "Testing of the hero is the primary dramatic function of the Threshold Guardian."

Threshold is defined as any point of entering, the line between here and there, also called limen. A liminal space is the time between the "what was" and the "next."

Any time you start a journey, whether across the state, into your book, or into the next adventure, you cross a threshold. Think of the age-old custom of the groom carrying his new bride across the threshold. That is a symbolic act of beginning a new life together, a new journey for them as a couple.

When you encounter a threshold, in the mythic sense, you also encounter a guardian, someone or something who stands ready to test you and the seriousness of your intent.

In a novel, as in life, there are many thresholds. During the journey of writing a novel, the High Priestess is often the first threshold guardian because she tests you at the deepest level, that of the spiritual or the unconscious.

She tests you to make sure you are prepared for the journey ahead (if not, she can help you prepare) and to help you understand that your writing has a sacred dimension to it.

For your characters, especially your hero or heroine, though not always visible, the High Priestess is there when your characters question their ability to begin, to break the first rule, to go through the first door, to step onto the ship, or to set forth on the Yellow Brick Road.

Vogler writes that "Successful heroes learn to recognize threshold guardians not as threatening enemies but as useful Allies. . . . Heroes also learn to recognize resistance as a source of strength."

Resistance for your characters, and you, can show up at any point your story.

The High Priestess is that first point of resistance, especially at the unconscious level where fears lurk in the dark corners and make you drag your feet once you've written the first ten to thirty pages.

That's when she enacts her next power or elemental quality.

Trust

A high priestess becomes a high priestess not just because she can lead rituals and can connect to her intuition, but because she knows how to work with the quality of trust.

As with the Magician and the power of focus for his audience and himself, the High Priestess has to create trust in others even as she has to trust herself to effectively and precisely read and act on her intuition.

Just as you need to trust your intuition about your story.

In workshops on dreaming, I am frequently asked about lucid dreams, those dreams where you know you are dreaming and can consciously act in the dream to change events in the it.

Dreams bring you information, guidance, and inspiration to inform and improve your life. (More about dreams in chapter 10 about the Moon card.) If you control the dream to suit your idea of what should occur, you might miss out on important information.

The same is true of your story. Sure, do your research. Plot, plan, and create an outline. But once you start writing, if you try to control the story, if you fail to trust it and the intuitive ideas that the High Priestess as Muse reveals to you, then your story could lose its vitality and impact, or you could feel blocked.

Trusting the story, trusting the Muse, is an initiation for you as a writer. If you can't face your fears and the negative messages your inner critic and the people around you may be sending you, then you won't cross the threshold from wanting to be a writer into being an author.

If you are a first-time writer, this is an especially challenging threshold. Talking about writing or your story, taking courses, or reading book after book on writing (just to make you feel safe) is NOT writing. Continue to do just that and you'll remain on the wrong side of the threshold and never publish a book.

Just as your story and hero and heroine will never go anywhere if trust and the willingness to confront the threshold guardian isn't there.

As with all the cards of the Tarot, there are positive and negative aspects to the High Priestess.

The positive aspects of the High Priestess for you, your story, and your characters are that she is willing to go where no woman (or man) has gone before, deep into the waters of the unconscious where mystery and the unknown lie. You don't have to labor and force the story, because she has the ability to reveal the secret wisdom, the secret stories behind the story, the unknown and the unseen, even if it takes a while.

She represents the spiritual dimensions of storytelling and your life. She also endows the gifts of intuition, clairvoyance, dreams, and visions.

Her challenge, especially for the writer, is that it's easy to get lost in her realm and be tempted to stay in the place of dreams and visions and imagination. But inner wisdom without outer action means you never finish the book.

The High Priestess is a valuable part of the fiction writer's journey, but she is only the beginning. Don't get stuck there.

The High Priestess's Questions for You

1. What simple ritual can you create to signify crossing a threshold into the sacred space of your writing?

2. What threshold guardians test your resolve to write (family member, job, inner critic)? Does it change your reaction to them if you see that person in this role?

3. Do you trust your intuition? Do you trust your story and your characters?

4. What is your deepest fear about writing this story? Your biggest dream?

Your Character as High Priestess

The High Priestess in fiction is Athena of Greek myth, Lady Galadriel in *Lord of the Rings*, Dr. Grace Augustine (Sigourney Weaver) in the film *Avatar*, or Yoda of *Star Wars*. All of them have the wisdom and the intuition to see deeply.

The High Priestess is the heroine who has to move out of her virginal inner world into relationship with the hero, or she serves as adviser to the hero or heroine. In her negative aspect, she is the know-it-all who believes she knows what's best for everyone and may try to manipulate others, even with an intent to do good, like Emma in Jane Austen's book of the same name.

Questions for Your High Priestess Character

1. Who in your story has the ability to see deeply, to tap into inner wisdom—your hero/ine or a supporting character?

2. Does she have an independent, set-apart virginal quality like an executive, scholar, recluse, or nun?

3. Is your character interested in the occult or things of a spiritual nature?

4. Does your character use their intuition and wisdom to help or hurt?

By now, you should be able to create several spreads for the High Priestess. A simple one would be a three-card spread for you or your character to represent

1. the High Priestess as threshold guardian,
2. one side of the threshold, and
3. what lies on the other side of it.

Don't get frustrated if you have trouble reaping any information from the cards at first. Part of writing—as in life—is the element of mystery.

The High Priestess invites you to trust anyway. Trust your intuition and deeper knowing.

Passion and the Rules for Travel

Donald Mass in his book *The Emotional Craft of Fiction* says that you as the novelist or storyteller are not writing to make readers feel as you do or as your characters do, but that you are instead "inducing for each reader a unique emotional journey through a story."

The Empress,
Tarot of the Sevenfold Mystery
by, and courtesy of, Robert M. Place.

The Emperor,
Tarot of the Sevenfold Mystery
by, and courtesy of, Robert M. Place.

From the very first page, in fact, from the very first paragraph, you must engage the reader emotionally. If you don't, you might as well be writing a school text—plenty of information but no emotional context. Passion and emotions are what drive your story. Structure and rules give form to that passion.

The Empress provides the emotional impact while the Emperor provides the structure and stability your story needs. Together the two compel your reader to keep turning pages long after it is time to go to sleep or get work done.

Empress

The Empress in early decks was illustrated and defined as the Queen, either the queen of a country, such as Queen Victoria or Catherine the Great, or the Queen of Heaven, and one of the names for Mary, the mother of Jesus. Over time, she became associated with some of the Earth and nature goddesses like Gaia, Demeter, and Aphrodite or Venus. Rather than a queen of power and position, she symbolized fecundity; that is, a prolific fertility, beauty, pleasure, and luxury. In her fecundity, she was Mother Earth, giving life to abundant forms in endless variety. As the Empress, her realm is Nature, and she gives and protects life.

Passion

A story is germinated in different ways—overheard conversations, news headlines or reports, dreams (gifts from the High Priestess), a what-if question, a desire to put a new twist on an old story, and more. But to actually write a story thousands of words long, you must love something about your story, have a passion for it. The passion keeps you writing in spite of the stresses of job, kids, bills, and whatever else shows up.

The Empress in her form as Venus or Aphrodite blesses you with her passion. She stands with the ship of your story and swings a champagne bottle against its hull, ceremonially launching it on its journey.

Before you swing the champagne bottle, ask yourself if the story has enough passion and pull, beckoning you with love and affection powerful enough to keep you sailing forward through storms and doldrums and mutinies. Because if you don't love it enough, chances are your readers won't either.

In a story, emotion propels and compels not only your story but your characters. Conflict arises out of the thwarted passions and strong desires of the characters.

In her passionate, sexual aspect, the Empress loves beauty and productivity and creativity. But she can also be overemotional, the drama queen, the sex kitten or the nymphomaniac, or the self-indulgent woman who expects her demands for pleasure to be met even at the expense of others. She's the one who will drive up credit card debt because she just had to have that coat, and that purse, and that ring. Like Hera, thwarted passions turn into jealousy and manipulation.

With passion there can be fertility and fecundity.

Fecundity

Is anyone more creative or productive than the Empress? She is abundant creativity, especially in her form as Gaia, the source of all life. As mother of all, she nurtures and nourishes.

Think of all the icons and paintings showing a mother with a babe at her breast—like Mary. The good mother is supportive, caring, encouraging, and protective. Rachel Pollack, in her book *Tarot Wisdom*, says that you are in the realm of the Empress as mother when you look at your sleeping child and "know you would kill to keep her safe."

Isn't that what we want for our writing and our stories? That we breathe abundant life into them, that we nurture them at each stage and step until finally . . . finally, they are ready to go out into the world.

With our characters, while we may not physically labor to give them birth, we certainly do labor to give them imaginative life. The challenge is to not be the helicopter mom, constantly hovering over them, but walking that fine line between providing support and love and keeping our hands and hearts and minds open so that they can walk their own paths.

Once you've created your list of characters (or at least your protagonist or protagonists and a few secondary characters) and are clear about some of their backstory and the motivations arising out of their emotions, then turn to the Emperor.

The Empress's Questions for You

1. Do you nurture yourself consistently in order to refill your creative well? How? Music? Art? Good food, or exercise and rest?

2. What are you passionate about in your story? How do you keep the fires of that passion stoked?

3. Do you put others' needs first with all your energies going to nurture them instead of yourself and your writing?

4. What do you do to gather the seeds of ideas and inspirations for other projects you aren't ready to work on yet?

Your Character as Empress

The Empress is the character who is nurturing and caring, the single mother who will do whatever she has to for her child. She might also be the woman looking for love in all the wrong places, searching for someone to receive her passion and meet her desire to be loved. She might be the girl next door, fit and with a love for the outdoors, or the guy more comfortable with animals than people.

She is the Queen of England or Daenerys Targaryen, dragon mother, from *Game of Thrones*. In her negative aspect, she is the wicked queen in "Snow White."

Questions for your Empress Character

1. Who in your story mothers others, either in a nurturing way or in a controlling way?

2. What role did your hero's or heroine's mother play in their beliefs or misbeliefs? Is the mother still an influence?

3. Is your Empress an environmental activist, passionate about her cause? Does he or she have a love of the outdoors or outdoor sports? Is she an actress, teacher, nurse, or queen?

4. Is your Empress character appropriately expressive or overly dramatic with her emotions?

5. How is your Empress fertile? With ideas, money, relationships, demands, her green thumb?

6. How does she rule others?

Emperor

As the Empress is the ultimate mother, the Emperor is the ultimate father. In early Tarot decks, the Emperor is an old man dressed in robes of authority, wearing a crown with an image of an eagle, the symbol of the ruling family of Europe at that time, the Habsburgs. He was the one who ruled and maintained the laws and structures of society.

Whether the realm encompasses rivers and mountains, or just parents and children within a home, the Emperor is the parent who establishes and upholds the rules. Even in the twenty-first century, the father is often viewed as the disciplinarian who metes out punishment when the rules are broken.

Because of a father's responsibilities outside the home, routines, schedules, and rules may be important to him. That reliable structure makes his duties and responsibilities easier to fulfill. And that brings us to the two words that express the essence of the Emperor and his role in your writing, your story, and your characters— structure and authority.

Authority

A definition of authority is the power or right to give orders, make decisions, and enforce obedience. That power can be personal or organizational, such as business or politics. But its origin in Latin, *auctor*, meant originator, promoter.

As originator, this puts the Emperor in very close relationship to the Empress because in order to originate life, you can't have one without the other.

But originator isn't just about creation, it's also about action, which is where the Emperor takes over from the Empress.

Much like the Magician, the Emperor has to have confidence in himself in order to exercise his authority. Whereas the Magician has to have confidence in his skills and his ability to be a channel for the energy of ideas and visions, the Emperor has to have confidence in his innate ability to influence and persuade others to action. He has to believe in the authority of his vision.

And isn't it interesting that in "authority" is the word "author"? An author isn't just an originator, someone who has the vision of the story, but also the person who takes responsibility for getting the story out in the world. You can't just want to sail the seas and explore the world, you have to take logical actions, make a plan, take steps to make the trip happen. The Emperor helps you be more businesslike in your writing because he knows that the desire to write and publish isn't enough.

The Emperor reminds you that if you want your story out in the world, you should start making plans now. Agents and editors will remind you that talking about your book and promoting yourself as an author begins early in your journey.

To establish your authority as an author who writes a certain type of book, think about how you promote and market yourself on social media, at social events, in your professional life, and in your community. Just as the Emperor (or kings) seldom go out in the world in disguise, don't you either. Wear the robes of your position. Claim your authority.

Which means that when you are asked at a party or other gathering what you do, you tell them that "I am a writer." And then when they ask you what you write, you say, "I am currently working on a (genre) novel."

Don't hem and haw about your writing, even if you aren't published yet.

Besides authority, the Emperor also offers structure and guidelines for the journey into your story.

Structure

In addition to rules and the laws and structures of society, the Emperor also represents the underlying forces, structures, and rules of nature (i.e., the scientific principles). As a balance to the emotions of the Empress, the Emperor embodies reason and logic, a let's-think-this-through approach.

With this approach, the number 4 is key because of the role of that number in life: four seasons or the four solar points of two solstices and two equinoxes; the four elements of earth, air, fire, and water (represented in the four suits of the Minor Arcana); the four directions of north, east, south, and west, and so on.

Four is the number of stability, organization, logic, commitment.

All of which you need as you prepare to write your novel. While a few successful novelists may have approached their writing career willy-nilly, for the most part, in order to write on a deadline, to actually finish first drafts, you want the stability of routines, goals, and commitments. All things the Emperor loves.

A novel needs structure, too. Pick up almost any book on plot or story structure and you'll read about the three-act structure, or the hero's journey, or Michael Hauge's six-stage plot structure. Every novel needs a framework just as every house needs framing and every human body needs bones.

So do your characters. They have backstories, beliefs and values, and experiences that provide the framework for motivations and actions.

The catch, of course, is too much reliance on structure and rules. New writers, new authors easily get so bound by the rules for scene or plot that all the passion of the Empress gets drained away. Be mindful of the balance between the Empress's passion and the Emperor's desire for structure.

In your story, the Emperor shows up as a strong leader in politics (think Margaret Thatcher), the military (Colin Powell), business (Bill Gates), or family. His positive characteristics are his ability to bring order out of chaos, to see the big picture, to provide security and stability. In his negative aspects, he is stubborn, authoritarian, controlling, a micromanager, rigid, and stuck in tradition and rules.

Questions for You as the Emperor

1. Are you prioritizing and planning your creative projects so that they get out into the world? Do you need to set regular planning time?

2. Do you need to organize your work/creative space in order to minimize creative chaos? How can you do that easily and quickly?

3. Do you have a schedule for writing, or are you just writing "when you can"? If the latter, does that need to change?

4. Are you clear about your destination, your goals, and your ambitions for your writing? What are you doing now to get you and your story talked about and known?

Your Character as Emperor

The ultimate Emperor in Western mythology is Zeus, showing both the good and bad qualities of the ruler. In Shakespeare, the Emperor is King Hamlet, whose death creates chaos in the realm. He is King Arthur. In *Lord of the Rings*, the Emperor is Sauron the Dark Lord (the negative aspects), as well as Aragorn. Odd though it may seem, he is also Martha Stewart, who, for all her cooking and decorating, which might make you think of her as Empress, brought strategic planning, organization, and authority to her career and business.

The Emperor can be the strong leader, the responsible father, like Tom Selleck's character in *Blue Bloods*, or the petty tyrant. He can be the community leader or the wealthy business magnate who fails to see the needs of those close to him. He can use the power he amalgamates for good or ill.

Questions for your Emperor Character

1. Who in your story acts as a father figure to others?

2. Does your Emperor character have a difficult time expressing emotions, preferring to talk about what is rational and logical in any situation? How does that affect his relationships, especially a love interest?

3. What are the biggest priorities or highest values for him (or her)? Is he looking for someone to be Empress to his Emperor, someone to help him build a dynasty and a legacy? Or is he just looking for relationships that highlight his image as Emperor?

4. Is he (or she) a warrior at heart, always ready for battle, determined to protect others whether they need protection or not?

5. If your Emperor is the antagonist, how does his need to exert power and control, and his inability to feel and express his emotions, challenge your hero or heroine?

To see an example of an Emperor spread for your character, see a three-card spread on him in chapter 16.

Before you launch out on your journey, you need a crew, a cast of characters, at least a few. And since the captain of a ship (an Emperor figure) was usually in charge of choosing the crew, the next chapter introduces the other royals of the deck: the Kings, Queens, Knights, and Pages of the Minor Arcana.

A Royal Cast of Characters

The royals of the Tarot, the Court Cards, usually indicate actual people in a Tarot reading. In your novel, they provide a great cast of characters and, regardless of gender on the card, can represent either males or females. The prime consideration for a character is the qualities of that particular Court Card. While the qualities here are mostly positive, when you are writing your story, think about how the opposite quality, or a frustration of that quality, might exhibit itself. For instance, a fiery young Page (male or female) could be all enthusiasm and readiness for action, but the negative of that might be someone who resents having to do all the fetching and carrying and in a moment of anger might start a fire, literally or figuratively, like Stephen King's Carrie.

When you start developing characters, shuffle just the Court Cards. Pull one card to represent a particular character, or intentionally pick a Court Card that embodies the energies of your character and then shuffle the rest of the Minor Arcana or the entire deck and pull cards to give you more insights and details about the character (see chapter 15 for an example).

Pages

Pages: The messengers of the court, usually a young boy or servant, in service to a nobleman from the time he turns seven years old. He runs messages, serves the nobleman at his table, cleans his clothing and weapons (not a small job if the nobleman is a knight), and learns the basics of combat. His term as a page is a form of education that trains him in the ways of the court and of combat.

For a character, think in terms not just of age but of vitality, energy, enthusiasm, and a desire to learn and advance. If you are writing a contemporary novel, remember that plenty of middle-aged and senior characters can have a youthful energy or enthusiasm that serves them well or gets them into trouble if they have too much.

The Page of Cups,
Tarot Grand Luxe by Ciro Marchetti.
Courtesy of US Games, Inc.

Page of Wands has a fiery nature, an eagerness that causes trouble because they are apt to be impulsive. They want something; they go after it. They have no or limited patience, and no ability to control anger.

Page of Cups has stars in their eyes, and big dreams that can be reasonable or totally illusory, depending on the person or persons who mentor them. They believe they are in service to a higher good, and woe betide anyone who forces them to see otherwise. This is the page who happily delivers flowers to his knight's lady one minute and mopes in a corner the next because she didn't smile at him. The mood swings of youth.

Page of Swords earns the sobriquet of whippersnapper. This kid (or childlike person) is smart—sometimes too smart. He or she sees things others miss, and often from a corner somewhere out of view of the adults. This page can put two and two together and come up with solutions that may be true but not always desirable. They twist words and answer questions truthfully but not completely. This page would rather notice than be noticed.

Page of Pentacles saves coins, clothes, stones, and bits of information, hiding them away against the time they might need them. He or she finds a use for things that others determine to be useless. This page loves animals and birds. He'd rather curry the knight's horse than deliver a missive to his lady. This is the page of ruddy good health or one who deals with some health shortcoming.

Knights

The Knight of Wands,
Tarot Grand Luxe by Ciro Marchetti.
Courtesy of US Games, Inc.

Knights: The hard workers who advance in their career by dint of training, service, battles fought and battles won, experience gained. A knight leaves the castle (home) to protect and serve, to go on a quest, and returns home again to bring back the spoils or rewards. He is older than the page but still energetic.

For a character, think about how that character serves others, and what he or she might be seeking or questing for. What rigorous training have they gone through? What sacrifices have been made in service to others? What drives them from home and what brings them back?

Knight of Wands, like the Page of Wands, tends to charge out and ahead on impulse, sometimes driven by anger or desire, sometimes by the need for adventure, and sometimes because his restless nature just won't let him stay put. This knight—man or woman—challenges unexplored, unconquered territory just for the sheer thrill and exhilaration of it, like a mountain climber. This is the character who needs to find a way to challenge his or her energy before settling down.

Knight of Cups is the romancing and romantic hero. His challenge is that he or she can get so caught up in the quest for ideal love that they miss the real thing when it crosses their path. This knight's high ideals of service can be used against them to manipulate them into actions they otherwise wouldn't take. He or she might be the tender-hearted introvert who uses their armor to protect themselves, making others around them think of them as coldhearted or unfeeling when the reverse is true. Often a dreamer, this knight needs a practical companion to keep them grounded.

Knight of Swords takes action for his or her own reasons, after thinking them through logically. Ideals are nice but need to be backed up by reason or they are useless. Give this knight a problem, a puzzle to sort through, and they are happy to come up with solution after solution. In fact, the many solutions generated by this knight make others dizzy, including himself. He wants to weigh the pros and cons of any situation to ensure that the decision made is the wise, logical one. But all that thinking about the problem can sometimes create a solution not of action but of inaction. The Knight of Swords loves argument for argument's sake and will debate laws and orders just to see what comes of it. This is the knight you want giving you the report of the venture or battle, because it will be clear and concise. Others see this knight as brilliant, sometimes arrogant, because he gets impatient with minds that can't keep up with his.

Knight of Coins is the salt of the earth, the farmer called away from his work to serve the realm in battle or other service. He'd rather garden, tend animals, or manage accounts than fight. If assigned a duty as a knight, he'd rather guard the castle or the realm's borders or act as bodyguard, sticking close to home. He or she is strong and not afraid of hard work and keeps his body, his armor, and his horse in top condition. A good companion for the other knights, he helps them stay grounded and practical, while they help him or her avoid becoming stodgy and set in their ways.

The Queen of Coins,
Tarot Grand Luxe by Ciro Marchetti.
Courtesy of US Games, Inc.

Queens

Queens: The mistresses of their elements or suits. They rule through inspiration, nurturance, and experience. In stories, these are usually adults but not only females. Sometimes, they are males who exhibit a different approach to leadership.

Queen of Wands is all passion, sex, and will. She is confident in her power and creative with the resources she has to hand. She (or he) is quick to anger but just as quick to give a deep belly laugh when something is funny. Cats follow this queen, loving her independence and her energy. In many decks, this queen sits on her throne with her legs apart, symbolizing her desires and sexuality. Sex is an expression of life and nothing to hide or be ashamed of. She would not be an easy partner, needing someone who is an equal and can satisfy her sexually.

Queen of Cups treasures the matters of the heart, whether that is creativity, dreams, healing, or relationships. When she gives herself in love it is with her whole heart and a strong sense of commitment and belonging. She is the mother who will fight for her children and those she loves. She is the one who will risk her life, making sacrifices for those she loves. She is the good listener, the one others come to for a hug, a tissue, and a shoulder to cry on. She makes a great doctor, psychotherapist, coach, or counselor.

Queen of Swords sees through trickery as if she was Superman with X-ray vision. If this queen's a woman, most men find her intimidating because she is so intelligent. She may operate from her brain most of the time, but she still has a heart and knows the power of words and the ability of them to cut both ways. Sometimes, she wishes she could control her tongue a little bit more. But whatever she says, she does not lie. She hates lies, always searching for truth. And for justice. Words are her coin and she can make a successful career using them as a lawyer, judge, mediator, teacher, or writer.

Queen of Coins, Earth mother extraordinaire, would rather be in her herb garden than sitting on the throne. Or cooking up a tasty treat in the kitchen of her restaurant. Her way of nurturing and inspiring is to feed and make others physically comfortable. She is the more personable manifestation of the Empress. Abundance in all its physical forms are her expression and her environment. Curvy of figure, fertile, connected deeply to nature. She likes pretty things. If she has the resources (and sometimes when she doesn't), she'll buy jewelry and clothes and accessories because she loves to feel and be beautiful. Her home is comfortable and welcoming, with lots of windows to the outside, and plants that bring nature inside.

Kings

The King of Swords,
Tarot Grand Luxe by Ciro Marchetti.
Courtesy of US Games, Inc.

Kings: Master of his (or her) element, power is his or hers to command. Whether through inheritance, struggle, or strategy, he's achieved his position and knows how to hold it, in business, politics, religion, and family. That also means that responsibility weighs heavily on his shoulders. One wrong decision, illness, or death, and the realm of the king's power could collapse. If age and experience brought maturity with it, then he'll make decisions that serve the well-being of his realm as well as his own.

In your stories, these are the people, both men and women, who seek to gain and use power, be it physical, mental, emotional, or spiritual. Think of someone like Donald Trump, Billy Graham, or Oprah, all people who reached the pinnacle of their fields and created kingdoms in the process. Sometimes, the king uses his/her power for the good of the realm; sometimes they use it for their aggrandizement and because power is their high.

King of Wands exudes power and confidence to the point, sometimes, of arrogance. They could stand to throttle back on their fiery energy to avoid burning others with their power and demands, especially those who aren't as confident or as driven. Once in power, this king is seldom satisfied with sitting back and ruling his realm. Rather, he (or she) seeks out new realms to conquer, because the adventure and the act of power is in getting to the top, not in being at the top. The challenge for this king is that if he grows his realm too large, he may burn himself (and those around him).

King of Cups has a tough time because as a leader he often has to suppress his emotions in order to rule and make decisions. That separation from his emotions leads to loneliness or isolation (lonely at the top). He may be the leader who sacrificed his own creative goals and expression to take on responsibilities he didn't seek out. Think of an actor like Robin Williams who was highly creative but in a constant battle with his mental and emotional monsters, a leader in his field who finally couldn't hide his emotional struggles any longer. Celebrity, which creates kings and queens, creates all kinds of emotional challenges that can result in drinking, drugs, and indiscriminate sex as a substitute for emotional bonding.

King of Swords is intelligent to the point of brilliance. Often, his or her leadership is expressed in fields like law, medicine, and politics. This is a king who uses words carefully and weighs decisions. He may often need reminding that not everyone can keep up with his thought processes. His ideas are often cutting edge, and he'll use his power and prestige to make those ideas a reality. Think of Steve Jobs or Elon Musk. Or, since Swords is the suit of communication (e.g., writing), consider George R. R. Martin or Joyce Carol Oates. And in the field of law and order, think of Ruth Bader Ginsburg and Sam Waterson's character in the television show *Law and Order*.

King of Pentacles is happily "in his counting house counting out his money." His wealth manifests not just in coin but in acreage or a large house, or in a large family. He offers no apologies for the abundance that his efforts bring him, but he is not stingy with them either. He likes sharing his largesse with others around him as a patron of the arts or a member of the board of trustees for nonprofits, who never fail to acknowledge him for his contributions.

Notes

OUT TO SEA

You've done all the prep work to launch into your story. You've identified your focus, stirred up your confidence, made a decision to trust your intuition and your story, braved up to the threshold guardian, connected to the emotions of your story, looked at structure, and identified some characters.

Now it's time to weigh anchor and leave safe harbor.

Who knows what you'll face once you've left harbor? No matter how many times you've made this trip before, anything could happen—and often does. This is why you have feelings of excitement and fear.

In the following chapters, you'll learn about the Major Arcana cards that will help you navigate deep and often-perilous waters. No doubt you will face storms and maybe even pirates and sea monsters, but if the Magician and High Priestess and the Empress and Emperor have done their work, you'll be prepared mentally, spiritually, emotionally, and physically.

That's a good foundation to travel with. Let's set sail.

6

Sailing with the Tide

It's time to sail away from the docks, out of the bay, and into deep waters.

To do that, you need to know how and when to take advantage of the tides, as well as knowing the hazards to avoid as you sail out of the harbor. You need the experience and wisdom of generations of sailors who have sailed from this shore before. Like the old salt who has been sailing these waters almost his whole life, the Hierophant knows or has access to knowledge and wisdom (tradition) and discipline you need to get the ship of your story from harbor to your final destination. And the Lovers help you make the choices and commitments necessary as you set course.

Hierophant

In early Tarot decks, The Hierophant was originally called The Pope, just as the High Priestess card was originally called the Papess. In both cards, the change in name reflected a movement away from the religious association to the more esoteric one.

According to Rachel Pollack, hierophant refers to the *Hierophantos*, the priest who directed the nine-day Eleusinian Mysteries. The word *Hierophantos* means he who causes to be seen—usually that which is sacred. At the time, knowledge was sacred, as were the traditions, governing structures, and laws.

The Hierophant and High Priestess are not just the male and female forms of the same energy. Instead, the High Priestess reveals the inner wisdom, the inner connection to the unconscious, while the Hierophant, or High Priest as it is called in some decks, reveals the outer wisdom of tradition, whether religious, societal, legal, or cultural (outside of the individual).

As an upholder and revealer of traditions, the Hierophant relates to the Emperor, supporting the Emperor's laws and rules, and vice versa. That's what tradition does, doesn't it?

The Hierophant,
Tarot of the Sevenfold Mystery
by, and courtesy of, Robert M. Place.

The Lovers,
Tarot of the Sevenfold Mystery
by, and courtesy of, Robert M. Place.

Tradition

It's easy to see how tradition plays a role in society, families, and religions, but what is its role in seafaring, traveling, and writing?

Travel and trade by ship were risky in centuries past. Language, myths, and rules arose to instill a sense of safety onboard. Tradition in the minds of the sailors was a means of reducing risks and increasing protection of the ship and its men.

The risks were considerable, enough so that maritime insurance for ships and their loads increased the farther from home dock the ships went, especially if a ship sailed alone. In the days before tugboats and organized pilotage, the difficulties weren't just in navigating the deeps but even navigating out of port because of the chaos of other ships, big and small, as well as poorly marked channels, and shifting tides and capricious winds.

You wanted to sail with someone who had experience, just as we want to fly on a plane with an experienced and mature pilot. The Hierophant provides maturity and experience for the writer and the story, understanding the flow of currents and tides, how to navigate by the stars, and even the rituals that help ensure safe and effective passage.

In your writing, the tradition of the craft provides you with plot structures and an understanding of what makes a good story. You have access to innumerable books on the craft of writing, and many writers who can reveal the craft's tradition and history to you.

Think of the Hierophant as a twinkle-eyed elderly librarian who can put his or her finger on any book you might need for your writing journey. He or she can even get you into the stacks or the collection of rare volumes and is delighted to help you with your research. Just be sure to put everything back where you found it.

The Hierophant is the mentor or coach for your writing, someone who is grounded in the craft, particularly in your genre, who will guide and inform while still allowing you to freely follow your own creative intuition. The Hierophant, like the Emperor, helps you create the discipline and rituals that will take you further along your creative career path.

For the story itself, tradition can serve as a theme, whether your characters break with tradition, especially religious and cultural traditions such as marriage, or rebel and start new traditions of their own.

A character shaped by tradition may be solid and secure in who he or she is. Or he could be a self-satisfied prig who's never stepped out of line in his life.

Beyond tradition that moves you safely out of harbor into the currents of your story, you also need rigor and discipline to keep writing. The Hierophant provides that with his inflexibility.

Inflexibility

While it may not seem like a desirable quality for either a person or creative endeavor, inflexibility has its place in a journey on the water and in words. Because there is no escape from a ship once it is on the water, it is a small world unto itself. Traditions and rules must be upheld. Any signs of disobedience or mutiny are quickly squelched . . . for the good of all. Flexibility is not a good quality for a captain. Like small children who need rules and structures and rituals for a feeling of security, so too do members engaged in a high-risk enterprise like sea travel.

In your writing, this means adopting an inflexible attitude about writing regularly, or continuing to write in spite of criticisms or discouragement from loved ones. Inflexibility keeps you forging ahead in spite of challenges or how much easier it might be to start a new story.

In your story, it means there will be a beginning, a middle, and an end with a conflict to keep you turning pages.

For your characters, it means that the inflexibility might be a good source of conflict in itself, a test for the hero or heroine as to how strong their commitment is, or if he or she is being too rigid, so rigid that their lives or well-being are threatened.

In Western society, one of the institutions that has an inflexible structure is marriage, and one of the roles of the High Priest, Pope, or Hierophant is that of celebrant for the marriage. Marriage, of course, is a social institution, performed by the Hierophant and supported and enforced by the laws of the Emperor.

Not surprisingly, then, the Hierophant is followed by the Lovers in the Tarot.

Questions for You as the Hierophant

1. What discipline or routine have you established to keep yourself creatively productive? Do you honor the sacredness and the value of your work enough to give it the time it needs?

2. What would you include on a small altar or in a sacred space to honor the tradition or legacy of writing but also to encourage and support you?

3. Do you need to attend a workshop or conference to enhance your skills, to understand plot, conflict, or story structure? Do you need someone to help you with the synopsis or plot of your novel?

4. Is it time to make friends with your local librarian? Perhaps spend more time in the library doing research on your subject?

Your Character as the Hierophant

The Hierophant in your story might be the powerful spiritual leader or father, or the religious tyrant. He's the hero who is determined to improve the lives of others through education or spiritual development or faith, or he might be the rebel who encourages others to think for themselves and not get sucked in by spiritual or religious snake oil salesmen.

Perhaps he or she is the character who is a spiritual activist on a mission who gets so caught up in it that they fail to see anything outside of the mission. Or he could be the devoted follower of a spiritual tradition, meditating regularly.

As the villain, he could be a spiritual or religious leader determined not to see beyond the rules established by his social or political leader, because of the personal power he gets in that position, even abusing his position to feed his own material needs.

The Hierophant is Merlin training Arthur (yes, he is the Magician too). In movies, he is James Dean in *Rebel Without a Cause*, or Sidney Poitier in *To Sir with Love*.

Questions for Your Hierophant Character

1. Who, in your story, is a spiritual leader or teacher? Is that person the hero or heroine, or a supporting character?

2. Is your Hierophant young or old, single or married, a professor, a priest or minister, an activist, a celebrant who loves performing weddings, or even a librarian who loves the knowledge found in books?

3. Is your Hierophant a powerful religious or spiritual leader, or is he a disciple of a tradition, struggling to believe? Does he have a hard time breaking rules, wanting to see himself as a good person, or is he a rebel, breaking rules because no one understands or thinks of him as good anyway? What does either position do to his relationships with others?

4. What is the biggest priority or highest value for him or her—faith, discipline, doing what's right, education? Is he looking for someone to establish rules, structure, and laws for him? Or is he looking for a High Priestess, who understands the importance of a spiritual life? Or is he sick of that and looking for someone who knows how to live in the moment, who is earthy, loves sex, and wants to be a mother?

5. If your Hierophant is the villain in the story, how does he use his spiritual power or the laws of his faith or country to control others?

Lovers

Pairing the Hierophant with the Lovers may seem strange. The first is about tradition and laws, while the second is about choice, relationships, and the chaos of love as symbolized by the impulsive, chaos-inducing Cupid on this card. But it is the Hierophant who brings order to the chaos by celebrating the commitment of marriage.

Writers often wrestle with the two needs of the impulsive, chaotic desire to create and the demands for structure and organization, as seen in the always-debated topic of pantsing versus plotting.

Like Death and the Tower, the Lovers card is one of those cards from the Tarot that shows up frequently in books, TV, and movies, usually in relationship to love or loss of love. However, originally, the card was about choice.

Choice

In early versions of the Lovers card, you see not two figures but three, usually two women and a man. The women represented lust and virtue (of course, it would be two women!). A dog, representing fidelity, walked with them. The card was about the choice the man had to make between lust and virtue. As a storyteller, you know that the story and its conflict lie in the struggle between desire (the short-term reward) and virtuous love and loyalty (the long-term reward). What do you want? What do you love?

A captain makes choices throughout the ship's journey, choices that are not always easy when they might mean the difference between life and death. But choices must be made.

You make choices at all stages of your writing journey—whether to begin or not, what type of story to tell, who your characters are, what your conflict is, and whether you will complete the story when you get bogged down. When finished, you choose how you will publish it or if you will.

Many choices to be made, but probably the biggest choice, the first choice, is whether or not to begin writing, to tell the story that spins in your head like a cyclone. Once you've made that choice, then, like the man in the card, the other aspect of the Lovers comes into play.

Commitment

In some early decks, like the *Visconti-Sforza*, and some later Tarot decks, the Lovers card had one man and one woman in the scene. Above or behind them is a Cupid with bow and arrow or a celebrant performing the marriage.

According to Robert Place in his book *The Fool's Journey*, this image is based on Renaissance betrothal portraits, a wedding picture of the happy couple. Marriage was considered the only way to tame the irrational and disruptive force of Cupid.

In the Rider-Waite-Smith illustration, and in other decks, angels or wings represent the presence of the divine blessing the sacred union.

A wedding is a declaration of commitment to love and to cherish "until death do you part." In most religious traditions, marriage is an important sacrament, defined as a ceremony that is an outward and visible sign of inward and spiritual divine grace. The commitment is significant and is supposed to endure.

As a sailor, stepping onto the ship and working to pull up anchor and raise the sails to get out of harbor, you make a commitment not easily broken.

As a writer, of course, you can always stop writing at any point in your story, unless you are under contract.

But if you love your story and yourself enough to make a true commitment to it, you are more likely to reach the end of your journey. If you sign a contract with an agent or editor, you've made another kind of commitment, even harder to break than the one to yourself. As you progress through your story, staying committed may be hard when you want to jump ship, but the inflexibility (Hierophant) of the commitment (Lovers) will help you keep working.

Other positive aspects of the Lovers are liberation, ecstasy, friendship, business partnership, compassion, the healing power of love, intimate communication, and a willingness to surrender to the power of love.

When the energy of the Lovers is distorted or abused, then its negative aspects are jealousy, adultery, dangerous liaisons, obsession, possession, separation, divorce, disharmony, sex without love, indecision, hard choices, lack of love, and looking for love in all the wrong places.

The Lovers' Questions for You

1. Do you love your work? Have you made a commitment to it? How do you follow through on that commitment?

2. Who or what is jealous of your relationship with your writing? How does that get in the way, or even sabotage your work?

3. What is the easiest way to enhance the romantic mood of your writing? Music, incense, candles, a fountain?

4. What do you do when you have a "fight" with your work? Do you place blame, take on all the responsibility, or find a balance? Ask questions like "Why isn't this working right now? What do we need to do together?"

5. Are you writing something you love? Or are you writing to meet the current trend (lust) of the market place? Is your relationship with your writing confining you or liberating you?

Your Character as the Lovers

The Lovers can signify a love story or be a symbol of an inner journey of choice, integration, and commitment for a character.

In fiction, the Lovers are Romeo and Juliet, Arthur and Guinevere (great love and also adultery), Rhett and Scarlet, and, of course, the whole genre of romance fiction. In the movies, they are Tony and Maria in *West Side Story*, Buttercup and Wesley in *Princess Bride*, and even Alex and Dan in *Fatal Attraction*.

Your Lovers character might be in love with work or career instead of a person. Or a character who thinks true love shouldn't have anything to do with lust but instead be a pure love, the knight's idea of love from afar. You can use the Lovers to write about any form of relationship—love, friendship, business, or even relationship with self.

When the energy is positive, the Lovers are more than just "in love." They love in way that transcends normal reality, usually resulting in a commitment—the couple about to be married, on their honeymoon, or just married, or always acting like young lovers. The Lovers might be a first, young love where wise choices give way to the ecstasy of the moment, or they might be the older, more mature love that has been tested by time and circumstance.

This card could suggest a love triangle, with an individual torn between the sensual draw of one partner and the apparent rightness of the other (for reasons of career, family, etc.) If the energy is distorted, the Lovers might indicate the antagonist who thinks he or she is in love with your hero or heroine but is really obsessed and driven to acts of violence or desperation.

This card, more than any other in the Major Arcana, is about relationship, so when it comes up, look at issues of relationships in your story.

The Lovers' Questions for Your Characters

1. Who are the people in your story that your character is in relationship with? By choice or circumstance? What is the quality of those relationships? Do they complement and support your character, or create conflict?

2. Is there a couple in your story? Do they lust after or love each other—or both? Are they making a choice in the relationship? Has love turned into obsession or possession?

3. If this is a love story, does it have a Happily Ever After ending? If so, how will you show that each partner is finally making a conscious choice to be in love and relationship with the other?

4. Is there sex in your story? Do the sex scenes strengthen the love relationship or threaten it? Is the sex transcendent or earthbound, merely an act of helping each other feel good?

5. What does commitment mean to each partner of your couple? What inhibits or undermines a willingness to commit?

6. Is there a character in your story who is so in love, so committed to his or her work, career, or service, that there is no room for love or a committed relationship? Is your character happy with the status quo?

7

Captain's Log

You've set out on this new adventure, writing a book—a new journey into the deep and endless ocean of words. It could be weeks, months, or even years before you type "The End" and step onto dry land again. It is daunting to gaze out to the horizon and see nothing but blank pages.

No card in these twenty-two Major Arcana cards says travel or successful movement through time and space like number 7, the Chariot. To drive that Chariot, racing along at top speed, you need card number 8, Strength.

The Chariot, *Tarot Grand Luxe*
by Ciro Marchetti.
Courtesy of US Games, Inc.

Strength, *Tarot Grand Luxe*
by Ciro Marchetti.
Courtesy of US Games, Inc.

Chariot

When you think of a chariot, you don't think of a slow procession from one place to another. No, you think of *Ben Hur* chariot races, or Helios racing across the sky with the sun.

Chariot implies speed, adventure, victory, and success.

Just what you want as you sail forth into deep waters with your story.

But driving and steering a chariot, just as with sailing a ship, is tricky. You have to keep your balance as the Chariot careens around corners on one wheel or bumps over rocks in its path, just as you have to keep your balance on the rocking deck of a ship, and through page after page of your story.

You also have to keep your hands on the reins (or the tiller of a ship) to ensure a successful arrival at your destination. If the horses pull in different directions, as they seem to on the card, the trick is to convey confidence and direction to them through the reins. Yanking on the reins to bring the horses to a halt is likely to cause a messy accident.

The Chariot teaches you how to be pulled along at high speeds while at the same time keeping your balance and maintaining your focus on your destination.

You don't win a chariot race by focusing on the other racers but rather on your own path, your horses, and by letting them pull you at top speed across the finish line.

Success

The word "victory" is often used in reference to political campaigns and sports competitions, like car races (another kind of chariot with horsepower). In business and elsewhere, the word "success" is more popular. But isn't it interesting that we also talk about "the drive to succeed"?

If you look at the Chariot in Ciro Marchetti's *Grand Luxe Tarot*, you'll see that the two horses pull the chariot at a speed that blows back the hair of the charioteer.

You'll also see that the horses are two different colors, one dark and one light, and they seem to pull in opposite directions, kind of like when characters take over a scene and pull you in a direction you're not sure you want to go.

The Chariot card reminds you to keep your hands on the reins and your eyes on your desired destination. What is the story you are telling? Which direction will best serve the story?

If you want momentum that drives you to success, then you need the will and determination to get there.

With the Lovers card, you said "I do" to your writing and your story. You made a commitment. In the Chariot, you call upon your will and determination to carry out that commitment.

Progress

What defines the success of a Chariot race? Or of any race? Progressing around the track for the required number of laps and crossing the finish line. Progress is movement forward or closer to the desired destination or goal.

That is what you want for your writing and your story—progress.

With a chariot race, laps and a finish line are measurements of progress that motivate you to keep racing. Aboard a sailing ship hundreds of years ago, progress was measured by sightings of familiar landmarks, or days spent at sea

Each episode of the popular television series *Star Trek* opened with the voice of Captain Kirk (William Shatner) reading from his captain's log.

Space: the final frontier. These are the voyages of the starship Enterprise. *Its five-year mission: to explore strange new worlds, to seek out new life and new civilizations, to boldly go where no man has gone before.*

The Enterprise was a futuristic chariot, carrying its passengers into strange new worlds, just as each story carries you and will, eventually, carry readers.

After that statement, Kirk always mentioned the Captain's Log and the star date as a way of orienting you in the time and location of the episode. The purpose of a captain's log was to note the passage of time and the progress of the ship, as well as to provide information for future voyages.

The keeping of the log, the ringing of the ship's bell, and the changing of shifts were routines that provided markers and signposts of the progress of time and the ship in the midst of an environment that was otherwise totally without them.

Goals and deadlines do the same for you as a writer. Your captain's log might be your writer's journal or a project planner. Set word, page, or time goals daily or weekly and keep a record of what you actually achieve. Other markers of progress might be scene cards that you turn over or a scene outline where you cross through scenes you've completed.

Questions for You as the Chariot

1. What is your WHY (your vehicle for success) for writing? What makes you want to keep at it in spite of friends and family who suggest you get a "real" job?

2. Do you expect too much from yourself and your writing too quickly? Do you need to slow down? Or are you dragging your feet, letting yourself get distracted and dissuaded from the story you are meant to write?

3. Do you wait for inspiration to strike? Or are you getting into your creative vehicle and flicking the reins by putting fingers to keyboard or pen to paper?

4. What routines ensure your success and mark your progress? Checklists? Rewards for reaching goals? Celebrations when you finally type "The End"?

5. What fuel drives your writing Chariot? Naps? Long walks? A healthful meal or snack? Just like the horses, you need food and rest.

Your Character as the Chariot

In myth, the Chariot is the vehicle that Hades uses to carry off Demeter's daughter, Persephone. It is also the vehicle that Hermes uses to return Persephone to her mother. In the movie *Ben Hur*, it is the chariot that allows the former wealthy Jewish prince sold into Roman slavery to become a victorious charioteer who rescues his suffering family. Driven too fast and without regard for others, the Chariot is also the business magnate narrowly focused on achieving power and status at the expense of personal relationships and an inner life.

If you think about the Chariot as success through daring and speed, then movies like *Top Gun* and *Days of Thunder* come to mind. In fiction, the Chariot can also be about journeys and travel, such as Bilbo Baggins in *The Hobbit*. In *Game of Thrones*, the dragons, fast and powerful, are the Chariot.

The Chariot's Questions for Your Characters

1. Does anyone in your story seem driven? By ambition? A heightened sense of responsibility to someone or something?

2. Is the ambition or responsibility worthwhile, or heroic? If so, why? If not, how does the ambition or responsibility limit your character's life? What will they lose if they continue in the current direction?

3. Does a character love to travel? How and where? Do they have any restrictions around travel? Does he or she travel to something or away from something?

4. Does one of your characters have "a need for speed"? Why? Where does it come from?

5. Is there anyone in your story who has a career that requires that quality of being just a bit of a daredevil? A mountain climber? A race car driver? An explorer?

As mentioned at the beginning of this section, driving a Chariot is not easy. To do it well, you need good balance, focus, and the next Major Arcana card in the Tarot, Strength.

Strength

At one time, this card showed a man, understood to be Hercules, defeating a lion by beating it with a large club. Not an image that most of us would want to work with. Fortunately, the Strength card is more often illustrated with a woman either opening or holding closed the mouth of a lion, or with the woman walking next to the lion with her hand on its back.

Both images of Strength represented one of the virtues, Fortitude. And fortitude is not about muscular strength but about inner strength, strength of will and heart.

Courage

As mentioned, in the *Visconti-Sforza* deck a man with a club stands over a downed lion. The card was not promoting cruelty to animals, but rather the strongman of myth, Hercules, and the first of his twelve labors, the task of killing the Nemean lion terrorizing the town of Nemea.

The tasks made Hercules the perfect embodiment of an idea the Greeks called *pathos*, which is virtuous struggle and suffering that leads to fame and, in Hercules's case, immortality (not unlike a writer's Herculean task).

Even though that card showed Hercules, it was not about his physical strength but about his fortitude. Fortitude is courage in the midst of pain or adversity. It is bravery, endurance, and resiliency. It is strength of heart and soul and mind rather than that of the body. Fortitude or Strength is also the virtue of any woman laboring to give birth.

In the Middle Ages and the Renaissance, Strength, also called Force or Fortitude, was one of the four cardinal virtues, the other three being Prudence, Justice, and Temperance or Restraint. In medieval times, Strength or Fortitude meant the ability to subdue or overcome one's passions or sexual desires (symbolized by the lion).

In the Rider-Waite-Smith deck, a woman has her hands around the jaws of the lion and is either forcing the lion's jaws open or closed. Or perhaps she coaxes them open or closed. In Ciro Marchetti's Strength card from his *Tarot Grand Luxe* deck, the woman stands with the lion in a position of companionship, her hands on its mane. Here, instead of a forceful strength of muscle or will, the card illustrates a harmony between human and animal, a connection to inner strength and confidence, to the desires and passions that can propel you to creative action.

The lion, after all, is Leo, the dramatic, creative sign of the zodiac.

The positive aspects of Strength, such as confidence, tenacity, endurance, courage, and harmony with nature, can be distorted. Then, abuse of power, cowardice, weakness, succumbing to one's physical desires, and a lack of stewardship for nature appear.

It takes courage to claim to be a writer in the midst of doubters and naysayers. Even more so in the presence of your own false beliefs about what a writer is.

It takes a lot of courage to embark on a journey you've never taken before. It also takes courage to set out on a journey you've taken before but that nevertheless carries extreme risk.

Years ago, every time a sailor set forth on a journey, loved ones hoped and prayed he or she would return, because even though the journey was known, the ocean and the weather were unpredictable. Pirates were always a threat.

Sallying forth into unknown waters takes courage and another aspect of fortitude: will.

Will

The captain of a sailing ship needs the same aspect of Strength that you need as a writer—the will to lead his crew, and to do so with discipline.

Although novels often portray sailors as having a love of the sea (there must have been a few), for sailors of centuries past the ocean was a fearsome place to be, especially because many sailors did not swim and many did not want their jobs. Often, they were conscripted to serve in the navy, or they inherited a legacy of fishing for a living, or because being a sailor was the only job available for someone of minimal skill and little or no education.

The captain often had a ship full of unhappy sailors, with mutiny a constant threat. Discipline was a necessary safeguard for everyone onboard, including the captain. Disobedience resulted in extra shifts, loss of privileges, or, for more-serious acts, floggings. Hopefully, you don't have to resort to such measures to discipline yourself and your writing.

The word "discipline" is enough to make anyone cringe even if you aren't a sailor. The term evokes images of school desks, knuckles, and rulers. But the root of the word is about learning, being a student and, as a student, surrendering to the teacher's or mentor's will.

For a writer, it is the exertion of will, exercising discipline, that brings you back again and again to your story until you type "The End." Setting writing goals, establishing a routine for your writing, and scheduling the time to write give the will work to do and strengthen it.

Logging your progress (the Chariot) encourages and motivates you so that you have the will to keep writing. If you fail to meet goals and be disciplined, make sure that your routines and practices serve your goals, then forgive yourself and get back to it. After all, the captain was not about to shoot a sailor for a misdemeanor. Good sailors are hard to come by in the middle of the ocean. Reward yourself when you follow through.

The woman on the Strength card needs no whip to keep the Lion in right relationship with her, walking at her side. All that is needed is a light touch of the hand, a connection that conveys respect, caring, and confidence.

That light touch is all you need to get you back at your computer or paper and pen.

The Strength's Card Questions for You

1. What scares you about writing your book? Are those fears real or imagined? What would happen if you faced them down?

2. What have you hesitated to write because you are fearful of what your family or loved ones, or your community or society, will think? Is the fear real or imagined?

3. Do you use all of the senses in your writing? That is, can your readers touch, taste, hear, smell, and see your story? Don't overdo it.

4. What is your greatest strength in writing? Is it character development? Plot? Description? Research? Theme? What is your greatest weakness? How can you strengthen it? A class, a book, a mentor?

Your Character as Strength

In myth, Strength is Atalanta, who outran suitor after suitor until Melanion won by distracting her with golden apples from Aphrodite. Later, Zeus turned them both into lions.

In fiction, Strength is Aslan in C. S. Lewis's *The Lion, the Witch, and the Wardrobe*. Strength is the country veterinarian, James Herriot, of *All Creatures Great and Small*. Strength as fortitude is found in the character Mattie Ross of *True Grit*, or Scarlett of *Gone with the Wind*. And remember *National Velvet*? In the story, Velvet Brown wins a gelding and trains the horse to win the Grand National Steeplechase. In the winning, she is the charioteer of the Chariot, but in the training of the horse, she displays love and determination, Velvet is Strength, and her name is an interesting play on that.

In the movies, Strength shows up as Princess Leia in *Star Wars* and the Cowardly Lion in *The Wizard of Oz*. Lion expresses the weakness of the negative side of Strength, and later, the positive side when he helps Dorothy go after the Wicked Witch of the North.

An exquisite example of the card of both fortitude and muscular strength is Charlize Theron's role in *Atomic Blonde*. When the movie opens, her character is bathing in a tub of ice water. When the camera pans behind her, you see scars, but also muscles rippling along her back.

Strength is the element of your story where your hero or heroine must prove that they have what it takes inside, to overcome, to endure, and to be successful.

Strength's Questions for Your Character

1. What role does fear play for your protagonist? Motivation? Limitation? Are the fears real or imagined? Is facing fear part of the character's arc? What does the character risk by doing so?

2. Is a character ruled by desire? What is your character willing to do to fulfill it? What are they not willing to do?

3. Does a character have a natural way with animals, as a nature lover or photographer, a veterinarian, an animal communicator, or even a shape shifter?

4. Does someone in your story abuse their power or strength with people or animals? Is there a backstory for that abuse?

5. Does someone have the characteristics of a feline—sensual, comfort loving, independent?

8

Entering Deep Waters, Seeking the Way

After leaving harbor, sailing away from sight of land can take some time. As long as land is in sight, the journey doesn't feel quite so risky. But eventually, the land sinks from the horizon and all you can see is water. The waters are deep beneath you and wide around you. Sky stretches overhead. The only safe place is the boat that felt so large when you first stepped aboard but now feels not much bigger than a bathtub.

As you travel into the deep waters of your story, strong undercurrents of uneasiness and doubt tug at you. It's just you and your characters out in the middle of nowhere. Now come the tests—and support—of the Hermit and the Wheel of Fortune.

Hermit

Although the current concept of hermit is a person who isolates himself for purposes of meditation and contemplation on nature or the Divine, in early Tarot decks, the Hermit represented old age and time.

The card showed an old man holding up an hourglass, as if to say, "Like sand through the hourglass, so are the *Days of Our Lives*" (cue music).

That old man was Saturn, the god of time and agriculture; hence his scythe and hourglass. Just as Strength from the last chapter represents the virtue of fortitude, the Hermit represents the virtue of prudence, a prudence influenced by the awareness of time and mortality.

The Hermit changed from the representation of time itself to the gifts of time— old age and wisdom. From there, the Hermit evolved into the sage, the philosopher, the solitary. Hermit derives from a Greek term meaning "one who lives in the desert." And with that idea of solitude, the hourglass became a lamp or lantern, signifying light that illuminated as well as serving as beacon or navigational aid.

The Hermit,
Tarot of the Sevenfold Mystery
by, and courtesy of, Robert M. Place.

The Wheel of Fortune,
Legacy of the Divine Tarot
by Ciro Marchetti.
Courtesy of Llewellyn Worldwide, Ltd.

Solitude

In order to get the big picture of your story and hear the whispers of your Muse, you might need to separate yourself from the noise and chaos of daily life and even your writing routine. For the sailor, the only place to go for quiet and the long view, even if it felt like a punishment (which it often was), was the crow's nest.

The crow's nest was a platform high atop the main mast of a sailing ship. From that platform, a sailor could spot potential hazards, the approach of other ships, or the appearance of land. Being that high gave the sailor perspective, the bigger picture of where the ship was relative to its environment. But the height exaggerated the motion of the ship, making even the most stalwart sailor seasick.

The high place for the Hermit is more spiritual than physical, a removal from the normal plane of existence to journey inward (perhaps under the guidance of the High Priestess). He withdraws—to the desert or the mountain or a retreat center. He searches for that transformative spiritual experience for his own enlightenment and to illuminate the way for others.

Writing is a solitary venture, and a need for solitude might seem redundant. But solitude is not just about being alone. It is about being alone in silence and surrendering to that silence to quiet the mind and listen for your inner voice, Muse, or High Priestess.

As seasick as the sailor might get from the crow's nest, the big picture was necessary. If you get a little light-headed thinking about going off somewhere for silence and solitude, remember that the results are worth it. And there will be light to illuminate your path.

Guiding Light

Lighthouses and other types of beacons were essential before the days of sonar and radar. The bright light beaming long distances from a high tower guided ships either into safe harbor or away from dangerous shoals and hazards like a fog.

Being lost in a fog is probably familiar to you, especially as you reach the middle of your story, and especially if you are a pantser without a plan or outline for your story. As you search the horizon for guidance, you wonder, "Where am I? Where do I go next with the conflict? What should my character do?" All you want at that point—desperately—is someone to light the way for you as you become more certain with each passing moment that you and your story will crash on the rocks.

Coaches, mentors, teachers, and other writers serve as guiding lights. But just as the captain and sailors used common sense, knowledge of sailing, and their instincts as they sailed toward that light, you have to use yours as well. Not every light leads you to your safe harbor. Some lights, intentionally or not, take you where you don't want to go.

Many a smuggler enriched himself by shining a light that led to shipwreck and the scavenging of valuable cargo. Be led by the light and wisdom of others but trust your intuition (the whispers of the High Priestess) and your experience to know what advice is right for you and what isn't. It is your story. So be discerning about the lights you follow.

The Hermit's Questions for You

1. How much time do you give yourself for imagining, daydreaming, contemplating? What keeps you from doing more?

2. Who are effective role models for your style or genre of writing? Who shines the light on the craft for you?

3. Where do you write? Do you need to find a quiet place away from everyone, or do you need to write someplace where other people congregate?

4. Do you go on writing retreats? Alone or with others? Do you ensure that there is quiet, alone time?

5. Do you have too much alone time? Are you too isolated and need to get out and socialize? Do you need to spend more time with other writers?

Your Character as the Hermit

Besides an actual hermit, your Hermit character might be a teacher, a guide in nature who takes people out into the wilderness, or a spiritual director. He or she could be a mountain climber who loves climbing both for the physical challenge and the opportunity it gives him for contemplation and perspective.

On the negative side, he or she could be someone who always finds themselves standing on the outside looking in, someone longing to be part of something, to belong, but who doesn't know how to go about it.

Perhaps your character is a college professor, someone who loves not only teaching but also mentoring students into new levels of understanding or accomplishment. Or it could be the professor who spends too much time in his ivory tower and doesn't want or know how to get out, similar to the writer or artist living in his or her own world of creation, who struggles to make the transition between that world and this.

The Hermit's Questions for Your Character

1. Is a character the loner, the lone wolf, standing outside society? Why? What will change that?

2. Is one of your main characters an introvert, someone who needs time away, quiet time for the arts, or spiritual work? How does that interfere with daily life?

3. Is a character isolated because of paranoia? Is the fear real or imagined? What caused it? Does your character imagine a course of action?

4. Is your character a retreat leader, a wilderness guide, a mountain climber? Do they have more sympathy for a tree or animal than a person?

5. Is someone in your story a high school teacher or a college professor? Do they have a good grasp of the world outside the school or do they suffer from "ivory tower-itis"?

While the Hermit originally represented time in personal terms of age and wisdom, the Wheel of Fortune is also associated with time and its passage but goes beyond the personal to the universal.

Wheel of Fortune

No, not the television game, even though the turn of that wheel could certainly make or break a person's fortune during the show's half hour.

This Wheel is the mythic wheel of time, the cycles of the seasons and seasonal celebrations, the cycles or rotations of the planets and stars as seen in the signs of the zodiac, the cycles of life—birth, growth, and death. This card represents fate and mortality, similar to the Hermit, but in the temporal or physical realm.

Time

In Greek mythology, the three Fates were the incarnations of destiny and life. Clotho spun the thread of life on her spinning wheel, Lachesis measured the thread allotted to that person, and dread Atropos cut the thread, ending life. Even mighty Zeus did not have the power to influence the timing of Atropos's cutting. The decision was hers alone.

Just as you alone determine when your story ends. But while you are still spinning the thread of your story . . .

Timing is everything.

Attending a conference when an agent you've never met before is there, and you both end up around a table of writers, sharing drinks and stories in the bar.

Encountering a writer friend between conference workshops and asking for information on a publishing house you aren't familiar with before deciding to pitch to them.

Offering a Tarot reading online, and the person who takes you up on the offer asks if you've considered writing a book on Tarot for writing.

Being a sailor or a captain on a ship means being aware and alert to the passage of time. You need to know if you'll have enough supplies to feed your crew before you reach your destination. You need to know the tides for departure and arrival in harbor. And you need to get your cargo to its destination on time or suffer fines or losses.

You know that you have to arrive in publishing port on time as well. Deadlines are a natural part of a professional writer's life. Yearly planners, calendars, and clocks cannot be ignored.

Unfortunately, for mortals, time does not go on forever.

That's not a bad thing. Time provides a framework—for your days, your years, your life, and your work. Think of how long it takes you to write a book. If you're a new writer, how fast are you writing? Then think of how much time it would take you to complete a book if there was no deadline, because everyone lived forever.

The Wheel turns. In many decks, like the Emperor, the Wheel suggests the importance of four—seasons, directions, and the stages of a person's life—a baby is born, grows into a child, becomes an adult, ages into an elder and dies.

A person and three animals, the bull, the lion, and the eagle, often hold positions on the Wheel. The human represents Aquarius, the bull is Taurus, the Lion is Leo, and the eagle represents the sign of Scorpio, the four fixed signs of the zodiac that mark the two solstices and the two equinoxes.

Time urges you to keep moving. It urges your characters, too, and can be a critical element in your story. Depending on your genre, that ticking clock increases tension and suspense (just as it does when your deadline is looming). A clock ticks away the seconds before a bomb blast, or the fuel on the plane runs low, or the deadline of a serial killer relentlessly approaches. Time is so important in some novels that chapters begin with the day or date and time. In George R. R. Martin's *A Song of Ice and Fire: The Game of Thrones*, even though seasons are much longer in the world of Westeros, "winter is coming," and that impending season impels much of the action.

Certain seasons bring rough weather, which can threaten a ship and its sailors—or character or writer. So, sailors did everything they could to minimize the threat by appeasing Lady Luck.

Fortune

Chance or luck is that external force that affects human affairs, for good or ill. The word comes from the old Latin, *Fortuna*, which was the name of the goddess that personified luck or chance. Vanna White, as letter turner on the *Wheel of Fortune* game show, plays the role of Fortuna, or Lady Luck.

If you look at Ciro Marchetti's Wheel of Fortune card from *The Legacy of the Divine Tarot*, you'll see above and behind the Wheel the planet Jupiter. In astrology, Jupiter is understood to be the big benefic, making everything bigger, but it usually indicates good fortune.

On the *Wheel of Fortune* game show, the winner goes home with a fortune and a new car or boat. At the roulette wheel (another Wheel of Fortune), a gambler could win or lose it all with a turn of the wheel.

On a ship, the helmsman steers the ship with the wheel, which on an old ship was connected mechanically to the ship's rudder. To change direction, the helmsman turned the wheel. In spite of rough winds and tides, the captain could determine the direction of his ship with that wheel and the positioning of the sails.

You are the helmsman of your writing journey. Though you may feel lost in a fog, or tossed by wind and wave, keep your direction in mind and your hand on the wheel.

If fighting the currents and the winds gets hard and tiring, then remind yourself that what goes up must come down, and vice versa. Just as the seasons turn and change, so also do the energies at work in your life and story.

Stuck periods don't last forever; however frightening they might be, the Wheel turns. When the up-and-down momentum of the Wheel gets to be too much, then do what the Hermit does. Get quiet and center, for at the center of the Wheel, motion is almost undetectable.

Wheel of Fortune's Questions for You

1. What are your creative cycles? What time of day—or night—is the easiest for you to write?

2. Do you respect the ebb and flow of your creativity, allowing for times of lack of ideas, words, or energy? Or do you keep cranking the Wheel, determined to push your work forward?

3. Who are effective role models for taking a gamble in your writing, your publishing, your promotion?

4. Do you create boundaries around your creative work? Are you clear about them with others? Do you hold them to your boundaries?

Your Character as the Wheel of Fortune

Any place a wheel, such as a spinning wheel or a roulette wheel or the wheel of a car or a paddleboat, appears, there is an element of Fortune present. Think of the fairy tale "Rumpelstiltskin," where the woman had to gamble on her future child in order to receive help spinning straw into gold. The spinning wheel also appears in "Sleeping Beauty" and is the instrument for delivering Sleeping Beauty to her fate. In myth, as mentioned earlier, it's the three Fates.

In the movies, the Wheel of Fortune is Doc and also the time machine in *Back to the Future*, when lives are changed by revisiting the past and visiting the future. It's also the James Bond movie *Casino Royale*. Or the bus in the movie *Speed*. On television, it is Dr. Who's phone booth time machine.

The Wheel of Fortune is the story element where your protagonists believe that they are the captains of their fate or struggle to become captains in spite of events out of their control, like Rocky in the movie of the same name.

Wheel of Fortune's Questions for Your Character

1. Does a character hold the fate of others in their hand, like a CEO or a king or queen? How does this affect him or her?

2. Does one of your main characters feel fated to do something (like take over the family farm)? How does that affect decision making?

3. Is a "ticking clock" in your story? Are you using it effectively to add tension and suspense to your story?

4. Is your character a potter, weaver, or spinner? Is he or she a climatologist studying the cycles and seasons? Or a gambler who plays the roulette wheel or bets at the racetrack (also a circle or wheel)? What happens because of the gambling?

5. Is your character the fulfillment of a prophecy, predicted to make a significant change in the world? How will he or she fulfill that prophecy?

9

Pirates and Sirens and Storms! Oh My!

This chapter looks at three cards: Justice, the Hanging Man, and Death.

Together, the three cards seem to tell an obvious tale of crime and punishment. A man goes to court for a terrible crime, is convicted, and is sentenced to hang until dead.

That simple story line evokes a variety of story questions. Was Justice served or miscarried? How heinous was the crime, and did the punishment fit it? Did someone administer their own justice? What role did revenge play in the crime or punishment?

The relationship of these three cards seems to lend itself to story more obviously than some of the pairs in previous chapters, but if you were doing a spread about your story and pulled these three cards, they wouldn't necessarily fall in this order. Playing with the cards and their order helps you play with your story and gives you more freedom around your writing.

What if the order is Hanging Man, Death, and Justice? You might have a story where, as a prank, some kids hang their friend by his foot upside down from a tree and leave him hanging (Hanging Man) and yelling? Hours later, he is discovered dead (Death). Who is responsible? The parents want the police to find out and bring the person to trial (Justice). In fact, the British television series *Midsomer Murders* has an episode with that story.

What if the order is Death, Justice, Hanging Man? Or Justice, Death, Hanging Man? Just by playing with the order of the cards, you see how many stories unfold, and not all of them are murder mysteries. Death isn't always murder, and as you will see, the Hanging Man and Justice have other aspects as well.

Justice,
Retrospective Tarot
by, and courtesy of,
Ciro Marchetti.

The Hanging Man,
Tarot of the Sevenfold Mystery
by, and courtesy of,
Robert M. Place.

Death,
Tarot Grand Luxe
by Ciro Marchetti.
Courtesy of US Games, Inc.

Justice

That's not fair! A child ever say that to you? Or yelled it yourself? What is the typical response? Life isn't fair . . . get over it. And yet, as humans, we long for fairness, for that balance that sees the bad guy punished and the good guy rewarded.

Justice was originally the eighth card in the Major Arcana. Strength was number 11. But because Justice's astrological sign is Libra, which follows Leo, the sign of Strength, and Virgo, which is the sign of the Hermit, the Golden Dawn Society decided that Justice belonged in position 11.

Appropriately, this card about balance, in this position, stands at the midpoint of the Major Arcana. Justice also represents one of the cardinal virtues in the Tarot.

What is justice? It's defined in the *Illustrated Oxford Dictionary* as just conduct, "the exercise of authority in the maintenance of right," and fairness.

In both early and later decks, Justice is a woman holding a sword in one hand and scales in the other. Behind or near her is a knight. In medieval times, the first rule of chivalry was that a knight be the embodiment of justice, carrying out the laws of the land and swearing to protect the fair sex. In Ciro Marchetti's *Retrospective Tarot*, Justice is represented by two female figures, blinded by their helmets while they weigh issues. The one with the scrolls represents the rules of law, and the one with the sword represents the means and authority necessary to enforce it.

On many decks, the sword points straight up as a symbol of commitment to honesty as well as the power of speech and of words; that is, what you say in court is expected to be the truth, the whole truth, and nothing but the truth. There are only three cards in the Tarot with a straight, upright sword: the Ace of Swords, the Queen of Swords, and Justice.

The scales, of course, symbolize what justice is about—bringing things back into balance.

Balance

What would the world be like if everything was in perfect balance, perfect harmony?

There would probably be no stories.

Stories arise out of conflict. They hold our attention (Magician) because of the tension of conflict. And conflict arises from an imbalance of some kind, an inequality of money, education, class, love, and more.

If your story has a happy ending or one that isn't tragic, then everything in that moment of ending is in balance, in harmony. The bad guy has been caught (punishment is implied), the heroine realizes she really does love that rebel hero, or the humans have finally escaped the aliens (or vice versa, as in *ET*).

An apparent disparity or inequality needs to exist between antagonist and protagonist for tension in the story to exist. The antagonist must appear to know more, have more strength, more money, more followers than the hero or heroine. Think of Sauron of *Lord of the Rings*, or Ares in *Wonder Woman*, seemingly all-knowing, all-powerful villains. How could they possibly be defeated?

And yet, two unassuming hobbits defeat Sauron. And it wasn't Wonder Woman's magic sword that defeated Ares. It was her love of a mortal.

Something always tips the scales back into balance. How the hero or heroine bring things back into balance is what makes the story and its ending intriguing or interesting.

Balance, as you can imagine, is important for a ship. Older sailing ships used sand or other materials as ballast for stability.

You need ballast to keep your writing process stable. Sleep, good food, time away from the work in long and short breaks, time with friends, and exercise all contribute to a writer's well-being and success.

Though you'd prefer to hole up in your writing cave and never emerge, you need the balance of stepping out into the world, engaging with others, developing new relationships, and nurturing old ones. Stories are born there as much as in your very fertile imagination.

You also need to balance accepted story structure with imagination, tension in your story with lighter moments.

And from that place of balance, you'll have the fortitude (Strength) to write the truth of your story.

Truth

"I solemnly and sincerely declare and affirm that the evidence I shall give will be the truth, the whole truth, and nothing but the truth."

This is the affirmation given by witnesses in United States courts. The affirmation is necessary for the court to know that the testimony coming from the witness is the truth (as he or she knows it), and for the witness to know that if he or she lies, there will be legal consequences. Because how can you hope to mete out Justice if you don't have all the facts or know the truth?

In court, cold, hard facts of forensics and other evidence are one form of truth, and witness testimony is another. Because one person's view of the truth may be distorted by stress, lapses in memory, and other factors, the more witnesses testifying, the better. Even then, it usually takes a panel of twelve jurors to winnow through all the testimony and facts to arrive at what they believe to be the truth.

Truth is often difficult to discern, in court or out. Think of Verbal in *The Usual Suspects* and the web of lies he so "truthfully" weaves for his interrogator. Or think of the unreliable narrator (someone whose credibility is in question) in fiction, such as Nick in the *The Great Gatsby*, or Huck in *The Adventures of Huckleberry Finn*.

Whether you use an unreliable narrator or not, truth is still an absolute necessity in your fiction writing. Seems contradictory, doesn't it, to think of truth in the same sentence as fiction? And yet, one of the draws of fiction is the ability to share truths within the pages of something you've made up.

The story has its own truth, its own integrity. If it lacks that, your reader quickly learns to distrust you. And that will be the last book of yours that they buy.

One of the ways to lose integrity in the story, to lose the bright sword of Truth, is to avoid the dark places of your stories. Write the pain, the loss, the grief, the hurt and disappointment, the jealousy, and the rage your story requires.

While you can make up the situations, the characters, and the settings of your story, the emotions need to ring true. If you find yourself uncertain of whether or not you are telling the truth, the whole truth, and nothing but the truth, then you might create a spread using the Justice card and asking the question "What truth in this story am I fighting to not see?"

Justice's Questions for You

1. Are you writing as often as you would like? If not, who or what do you blame? If you were asked to testify in court about this, what would your "whole truth" be?

2. Do you create artificial rules around your work, such as you can only write after you put the kids to bed, or finish writing that report for a client, or do the laundry? If you made the rules, you can change them. What self-imposed rules need to be changed?

3. Are you your harshest critic when you review or edit your work? Is that a good thing?

4. Do you dare to write the truth of your story? What would help you brave up?

Your Character as Justice

In Greek myth, Themis is the goddess of justice, viewed as the personification of law, including natural law, and that fairness that children seek. Naturally, her symbol is scales. Maat was the goddess of truth and justice in Egyptian mythology. She weighed a dead person's heart against a feather to determine if that person deserved a trip to the desired afterlife or not.

One of the best examples of Justice in fiction is the Pulitzer Prize–winning novel *To Kill a Mockingbird*, for both the trial and its hero, the lawyer Atticus Finch. And, of course, Justice shows up in most mystery and suspense novels, ensuring that the criminal is caught and punished.

In movies, Justice appears in *A Few Good Men* as Navy lawyer Danny Kaffee, who leads the defense in a court martial for two Marines accused of murdering a fellow Marine. Appropriately, this is the film where the colonel played by Jack Nicholson tells Kaffee (Tom Cruise), "You can't handle the truth!"

On television, Justice is all those crime shows like *Law & Order*, *CSI*, *NCIS*, and others. The issues of right and wrong, justice and injustice, and the balance between mercy and punishment are themes that undergird the shows.

Justice's Questions for Your Character

1. Does anyone in your story play the role of truth seer, truth seeker? How do others in the story react to that person? Does the role isolate him or her?

2. Is there something in the past of one of your characters that's created a belief that dictates the life path? Who is blamed for that? How does that affect the relationship if there is one? What does the character not see about the truth of that event?

3. Is your character someone who never seems to accept responsibility but always blames everyone else? What does that lead to?

4. Is your character a lawyer, a judge, or even a lawmaker? How much power over others do they have? How does that warp or strengthen that character? Do they understand about the balance between mercy and severity?

5. Does a character believe laws and rules are for sheep, that someone of his or her intelligence, class, or economic power doesn't have to abide by the laws meant for the common man? What helps him or her see the Truth?

6. Does someone in your story break the law for the thrill of it? Is your character someone who is outside the law because of a special role, like an undercover agent?

Hanging Man

Sometimes, to truly see or to see what you haven't before, you need a new way of looking at things. You need to be turned upside down.

Like the Hanging Man.

Hanging is an ancient form of punishment. On ships, hanging was reserved for the worst crimes, such as treasonous acts. In a world confined to the hull and masts of a ship, punishment—and Justice—was swift and sure. The hanging itself was slow, and the crew were called to witness it as a way of ensuring that they maintained onboard discipline.

The popular name for this card in Renaissance Italy was "il Traditore," the Traitor. Robert Place, in his book *The Fool's Journey*, says that at that time, artists were often hired to depict politicians in the position of the Hanged or Hanging Man to suggest that they were traitors.

Caravaggio, an artist painting from 1590 to 1610, painted *The Crucifixion of St. Peter*, showing Peter hanging upside down since he denied (i.e., betrayed) the Christ three times. Related to that, you will often see coins falling from the pockets of the Hanged Man, which harken back to the coins paid to Judas Iscariot for betraying Jesus to the Roman soldiers.

But the Hanged Man is not always punishment. Rachel Pollack says that the Hanged Man, in many cases, does not looked distressed by his position, suggesting that something more is going on besides treason and execution.

This upside-down position is also the usual position in which a baby emerges into the world—head first, with that umbilical cord anchoring her to something bigger and more powerful.

Then what is the Hanging Man about?

Initiation

Hanging upside down is an act of initiation and surrender, especially in shamanic traditions. What happens when you hang upside down? Blood flow to the brain increases, as do the oxygen levels, which helps the brain function better, improving concentration, memory, and clear thinking. Increased oxygen could also account for states of ecstasy reached in that position, provided that the person doesn't hang upside down too long, because too much blood to the brain is damaging.

A myth about the Norse trickster god, Odin, who had an unquenchable thirst for knowledge and wisdom, relates that in order to receive the wisdom of the runes (a magically charged Germanic alphabet believed to contain the secrets of the Universe), the god allowed himself to be hung upside down on the World Tree for nine days. Imagine the discomfort, the agony, even the frustration of those nine days.

Nevertheless, as tricky as he was known to be, with his focus on alphabets, wisdom, and knowledge, he sounds like a good patron god for writers. Especially when you are feeling the frustration of being surrounded by story fog or are becalmed in the middle of an ocean of words.

What is needed is a new perspective, similar to what you may have experienced as a child when you lay back on your bed with your head hanging over the edge so that your room appeared topsy-turvy.

Surrender

As mentioned, the upside-down position of the Hanging or Hanged Man is the position of birth—and rebirth. Initiation rituals often include a stage of imitating birth in order to symbolize the rebirth of the initiate into a new way of being, as a newborn member of a group or tradition.

In actual birth, both infant and mother must surrender to the process. They can do nothing (without medical interference) to change what has seized them both. While the baby may not understand what is going on, the mother certainly does, and the feeling of inevitability is one she can either fight or surrender to.

In your novel, especially in that challenging middle, the impulse is to push harder on the writing in order to speed things along. Let's get this book baby born! Instead, this may be where you need to model Odin. Allow your story, your characters, and yourself to be turned upside down. Surrender to the initiation that is happening so that new insights are received.

If you ask twenty women how long their labor lasted, you will get twenty different answers. It takes as long as it takes. Drugs can hurry the process, but that generally just makes the labor more intense, more painful, or uncomfortable. The best thing to do is . . .

Breathe. Surrender to the process.

Soon the winds will blow away the fog and you'll be full sail ahead.

Hanging Man's Questions for You

1. Are you hung up in your writing? Is the block one you need to surrender to in order to gain new insights into your process or story?

2. Do you take time away from your writing to relax, refresh, and renew? When was the last time you went to a movie or museum, or took a trip more than a half hour from home to gain new perspectives?

3. Do you need to practice patience with your writing, your life, your agents, or your editors? What is behind your desire to hurry up?

4. What if you turned your writing process upside down? Write at a different time. Write in a different place. Use the computer instead of paper and pen or vice versa. Sometimes change is all that is needed for new perspectives.

5. What initiation is happening as you write this book?

Your Character as the Hanging Man

The Hanged or Hanging Man (or Woman) is every hero/ine who has been overcome by the bad guy and, as they wait for death or violence, realize what they wouldn't admit before—that they love the other.

It's Dorothy in the *Wizard of Oz* when the Wicked Witch has her locked up in her tower awaiting death, and Rapunzel, locked in her tower, awaiting freedom and life.

In the movies, the Hanging Man is both Jack and Joan in the *Jewel of the Nile* (the sequel to *Romancing the Stone*), suspended by ropes over a deep pit. Jack's rope is soaked in goat's blood, making rats chew frantically at the rope, and Joan's rope is wearing slowly away from drops of acid. While they hang there, although not upside down physically, emotionally their world has turned upside down, giving them new perspectives on their relationship.

Or it's the movie *Adam*, about a young man living with Asperger's syndrome, a form of autism. While he's not bound or suspended physically, his mental condition keeps him suspended in an almost-childlike state.

A favorite Hanging Man technique on television, especially soap operas, is the coma that a character is thrown into, providing new perspectives for the patient and those who care for him or her.

The Hanged Man's Questions for Your Character

1. Does anyone in your story play the role of martyr or victim as a form of manipulation? How do others in the story react?

2. Is one of your characters a daydreamer, someone who lacks direction and motivation and never seems to grow up? Does the character live with a partner or parent who is more caretaker than anything else?

3. Is there a theme of being different in your story? Different how—disability, work, race, gender, education, income? What does that do to that character's perspective on life? How can that change?

4. Is your character an alternative healer, astrologer, Tarotist, psychic, or someone else whose career is outside the norm? What have they had to sacrifice for that work?

5. Has one of your characters been captured and bound by the bad guys? What does that do to his or her sense of self? Perspectives on life and relationships? How does he or she get free?

6. What ultimate sacrifice of something important must the hero or heroine make in order to achieve something suddenly deemed of more worth?

7. What has your character done that gets him or her accused of being a traitor—rightly or wrongly?

Death

Even if you've never picked up a Tarot deck or had a Tarot reading, you've probably seen this Tarot card show up in a movie, such as the James Bond film *Live and Let Die*. The card reader turns up the card and—cue the menacing music—there is the Death card.

In films or television, the title of the card is taken literally. It always threatens death, either for the querent or someone close to them.

Of course, the Tarot is often literal, and one look at this card from Marchetti's *Tarot Grand Luxe* is enough to give anyone shivers. But there are all kinds of deaths, not just physical ones.

James Scott Bell, in his book *Write Your Novel from the Middle*, says, "A great novel is the record of how a character fights with death." For him, that death comes in one or more of three ways: physical, professional, or psychological.

Death is an ending—relationships, careers, popularity, and dreams can all die.

While most Tarot readers would not tell clients that physical death is imminent, there is no reason someone in your story can't do that, especially if they have no scruples. It has been done frequently in movies and television, though, so be careful how you use it. Why use it? To invoke tension in the story, like that scary music in *Jaws* that always alerted you to the (shudder) appearance of that Great White.

In other words, to evoke that sure-to-capture-your-attention emotion: fear.

Fear

One of the biggest fears of a ship's crew was pirates. Spying a pirate ship meant battle, probably to death or slavery, along with the loss of valuable cargo. Before fighting, though, they would first try to outrun the pirates. Even today, pirates still threaten certain shipping lanes of the ocean, turning what should be a mundane voyage into one of calamity as in the Tom Hanks movie *Captain Phillips*.

For you on your writing journey, fear is the pirate that can steal your story or sink it to the ocean floor.

A famous *Peanuts* cartoon shows Linus sitting at Lucy's psychiatrist booth. He admits to her that he is in sad shape, full of fear and anxiety. Lucy lists a series of possible conditions like fear of cats, fear of responsibility, and so forth. Then she suggests he has pantophobia, the fear of everything. "That's it!" Linus shouts, knocking Lucy off her seat.

The biggest fear for most people is death. Some people won't get a Tarot reading because they are afraid that the Death card will show up.

Fear of death can block your writing. No, not the death where you keel over while writing, but the death of hopes and dreams of success, of sales, and of telling a good story. The deathly fear you have to overcome every time you look at that blank page or screen. Or when you reach the middle of your story and you don't know what to write next. Or when you've published the first or second or third book and wonder if there are any more books in your brain.

Failure is a kind of death. Sitting down to write a novel, and continuing to do so, often feels like standing at the edge of the precipice. Like the Fool. Stepping off seems like the worst idiocy. Death lurks, right? That skull and crossbones flaps in the wind, threatening you, especially as you get closer to safe harbor.

Just remember that death, big and little, is about letting go—of expectations, beliefs, attitudes, ego. All of that.

Can you let go of your fears and your ego enough to let the story live?

Because there is a gift in letting go, as any organizational expert will tell you. You'll have room to breathe, room to move, room for new beginnings.

Endings

Is there anything more satisfying than getting to the last page of your manuscript and typing "The End"?

Well, sure, there are a few things, but that sense of accomplishment is huge. The story you've been lugging around forever is finally complete. Yay! Time for a celebration, right?

Uh, maybe not. After all, you've lived with those characters and their challenges and triumphs for months, maybe years. And now, you're supposed to watch them sail happily off into the sunset?

Some writers get blocked in the middle or close to the end of their books because they don't want to let go. Letting go means that if they want to do more than shove it in a drawer, they have to send it out to be judged by agents and editors. Or they have to publish it themselves and then brace for readers' reactions.

Writing "The End" means you have to say goodbye to the characters you've lived with for so long, but it also allows you say hello to new characters, new stories.

Book series arise because authors and readers fall in love with characters and settings. But the longer the series continues, even for skilled writers like Janet Evanovich (the Stephanie Plum mystery series) or J. K. Rowling (the Harry Potter series) or others, the energy, the interest, and the life of the series get more challenging to maintain.

Because, as the fate Atropos teaches, everything has an ending.

Including your stories.

Including professional relationships.

After attending years of conferences and listening to well-published writers talk about agents disappearing and contracts ending unexpectedly, I know that Atropos is always present with her scissors. And sometimes, no matter how you plead and bargain, she will cut.

But the Death card does not appear at the end of the Fool's journey, did you notice?

It appears closer to the middle.

Because Death offers a new stage, a new beginning, in your writing, your story, or your characters' lives.

And sometimes Death isn't the scariest thing you'll face as a writer on your journey.

Death's Questions for You

1. Are you working and reworking a current writing project, hoping to make it perfect? Do you need to let it go? Either out into the world or into a drawer, so you can start a new project?

2. What habits or old ways of doing things in your personal life or your creative process do you need to be let go of or let die, in order for your creativity to bloom?

3. Are you afraid to visit the dark places of your creative work, the places where Death and other scary things reside? Does that limit the quality and depth of your work?

4. Is fear of the death of your hopes and dreams for your writing keeping you from writing? What is the worst thing that could happen? How would you deal with that? Would you still write?

Your Character as Death

Death is a central figure in *Hamlet* as Hamlet seeks out his father's murderer. Death is the third ghost in Charles Dickens's *Christmas Carol*. He is Mordor and Sauron in J. R. R. Tolkien's ring trilogy. Dickens seemed to love Death because he also makes an appearance as Miss Havisham in *Great Expectations*. Jilted at the altar, she wears her wedding dress every day and leaves the wedding breakfast and cake uneaten on her table, her wedding dreams as dead and dusty as the food.

In the movie *The Blue Butterfly*, Death stalks the terminally ill ten-year-old boy who stalks the most beautiful butterfly on Earth, the mythic and elusive Blue Morpho (Morpheus being the Greek god of dreams). *What Dreams May Come* shows a man who dies and has to learn how to live his life after death. And in *Snow White and the Huntsman*, the wicked queen tries to stave off her aging and death by draining the life from others.

Death visits television frequently on soap operas (both in sex—the little death—and actual physical death), on mystery and suspense shows, and on crime and law shows.

Death's Questions for Your Character

1. Does someone in your story act as Death, ending events, projects, people, or groups? How do others react to that person?

2. Does a main character risk death for the life of another—for love, heroism, duty, or a lack of desire to live? How does that risk change your character? What does it teach him or her about the value of life?

3. Is a character in late middle age, seeing old age and death approaching? What is their response? Denial, sexual liaisons, or a struggle to accept?

4. Is Death a theme in your story? What is ending? What is beginning?

5. Is your character a minister, an undertaker, a funeral director, a hospice caretaker, or even a spy, regularly dealing with death? How does that affect them?

6. Is one of your characters a murderer, especially a serial killer, someone fascinated or obsessed by watching others die? How did the obsession originate? What do they teach the other characters in your story?

7. If your story is mythic or a fantasy, is one of your characters a gatekeeper for Death? A minion of Death? Or someone who helps others make the passage from Life to Death?

10

Davy Jones Locker and the Monsters That Lie Beneath

Reaching the end of your first draft is not the end of your writing journey but somewhere just past the middle. While you may sense that the end of the journey will soon be in sight, now is not the time to get lazy.

Just as the captain makes sure the crew gets the ship safely into harbor, you have to finish, edit, and polish that first draft, not just once but several times at least. Writers talk about doing anywhere from three to ten rounds of editing so that the draft that is finally sent off either to an editor or, if self-publishing, to a formatter and distributors, is finely polished—and very different from that rough first draft.

None of these tasks of writing—finishing, editing, and polishing—is a breeze. Some writers enjoy the process while other writers hate it because it is tedious work. Still, being mindful and committed to this part of the journey makes all the difference, because there are monsters just waiting to rise up and capsize your ship or sink it beneath the waves.

And it is here in the finishing, editing, and rewrites that the next three cards, Temperance, the Devil, and the Tower, help you move closer to your book's destination.

Temperance

In *Tarot Wisdom*, Rachel Pollack says this card has never been a favorite because it didn't seem all that interesting or exciting, especially as it originally represented one of the four cardinal virtues. She changed her mind about it when she noted that in many versions the angel in the card has one foot on land and one in water, indicating "a mingling of the inner life and action (something that often concerns writers)."

Temperance,	The Devil,	The Tower,
Tarot of the Sevenfold Mystery	*Legacy of the Divine Tarot*	*Tarot of the Sevenfold Mystery*
by, and courtesy of,	by Ciro Marchetti.	by, and courtesy of,
Robert M. Place.	*Courtesy of Llewellyn*	Robert M. Place.
	Worldwide, Ltd.	

Robert Place, as well, mentions in his book *The Fool's Journey* that Temperance represents not the denial of desire, but the being able to satisfy "desires in a way that is healthy and beautiful. It is the virtue of the musician and the artist and allows them to create balance and beauty in their work."

Temperance comes from the Latin *temperare*, which means to mix and bring into harmony two or more opposing or different elements, a blending of opposites.

The card became one of my favorites when I used *The Druidcraft Tarot* by Will Worthington (illustrator) and Philip and Stephanie Carr-Gomm. In an explanation of their Temperance card, they refer to a favorite goddess of mine, Brighid.

In most decks, you see Temperance working to balance, in some way, the two elements of water and fire. Too much water can extinguish fire, and too much fire can evaporate water. But with the skill and knowledge to use both, the glassblower creates something beautiful in its fragility, and the blacksmith shapes a hard-wearing shoe for a horse or hones a sword for a king.

Desire

Brighid is the goddess of the well. For those without access to running water, water is a precious resource. Communities were created around wells and springs or near rivers, for water nourishes the body and community just as emotion nourishes your story.

Centuries ago, before books and reading, people relied on the traveling storytellers or bards. Stories were shared as entertainment as well as education and history. The stories could be gruesome and bloody, heroic or funny. But, like your story, they had to evoke emotion or their audience would get up and wander away—without leaving coins in the bard's cup.

Emotion, as I've mentioned elsewhere, is one of the most important elements of your story, not just in your story but for your story. You must desire to see that story on page or screen enough to spend the hours of work necessary to get it written. Your audience has to desire to know what happens next in order to keep reading (or watching or listening).

As you reach the ending stage of your story—the Black Moment, climax, and resolution—you not only have to maintain the emotional energy of your story, you have to increase it as you approach the climax, so that the ending induces an emotional sense of completion in your reader. In the editing process, you have to keep that water element alive in each successive draft. Not so much water that your scenes become melodramatic, but enough water to keep your readers from feeling parched for connection.

In the Minor Arcana, the suit of Cups (that hold water) represents the realm of the heart, so the desires here are the ones that are the yearnings of the heart, which is different from the fiery passions, will, and desires of the suit of Wands. Temperance holds both: desire and passion.

Passion

Brighid is also the goddess of the forge, the place of burning heat and drenching sweat.

In a blacksmith's forge, a hot fire is essential for heating metal so that it is soft enough to hammer into shape, or to hammer out imperfections.

As editor of your story, whether first draft or fifth, you are the blacksmith, hammering your writing into shape, smoothing any rough edges until your story is as bright and sharp as it can be.

To temper a sword after its desired length and sharpness have been achieved, the sword is heated again and then left to cool naturally in the air. Just as you have to do with the editing process. Unless you are a multi-published, highly experienced writer, you need to go through multiple edits of your manuscript before you submit, and again after a publisher has purchased your story. You're likely to reach a point where you'll need to cool off as much as your manuscript does, because editing is hard, sweaty work.

In the process of editing, remember the theme and the heart of your story. You don't want to lose that while you craft better sentences and scenes. But you also don't want to lose the heat of your story, because passion as much as desire motivates human action. Love and lust, for example, can exist at the same time and obviously motivate many a hero or heroine.

Temperance shows you how to balance both aspects, so that you and your story emerge stronger, prepared for the challenges of the Devil.

Temperance's Questions for You

1. How can you use the water of creative inspiration to strengthen that which is heated and forged in the fire?

2. Do you constantly work and produce but feel like your love for your work and your inspiration has dried up? How can you refill your creative well?

3. Do you spend too much time daydreaming about an idea or get halfway done on one project only to lose steam? How can you add a little fire (passion that shapes with will and discipline) to the water?

4. As you finish your first draft and begin to edit, what do you need to do to keep both the water and fire balanced? Start a new project? Ask for or hire editorial or content development assistance?

Your Character as Temperance

In some decks, this card is actually called Creativity, because of that act of combining elements in unusual ways. James Wanless's *Voyager* deck calls this card Art. The arts require a balance between fire and water, passion and desire. A ballerina, for example, has to have the heart's desire, the dream of dancing balanced with the very strong passion and will to practice and practice in order to succeed in a very competitive world.

If your character is in a creative field, he or she must be willing to be tempered. The fiery excitement of success is often cooled by the tears of disappointment.

Your protagonist could be an artist or craftsperson, or someone who likes to work in a lab mixing elements together for a new scientific breakthrough, or a chef in the kitchen using fire and water to create amazing dishes.

Temperance also refers to avoiding an overindulgence in things like drinking and eating, so your character could be challenged by weight, alcohol, drugs, or sex, or they abstain totally. Your character might need to control his temper and even need anger management, as in the movie by the same name starring Adam Sandler and Jack Nicholson.

On television, Temperance shows up in cooking shows like *Chopped* (where contestants both flare up and cry), and *American Idol*, where contestants' tempers (both anger and creative strength) are constantly tested.

In fiction, Temperance is Heathcliff in *Wuthering Heights*, whose fiery temperament destroys him, or Captain Ahab in *Moby Dick*, whose passion to defeat the white whale is thwarted by the waters that surround him and the animal who is so comfortable in them.

Temperance's Questions for Your Character

1. What character has the biggest challenge with temper? Keeping it? Losing it (because sometimes losing temper is necessary for a situation to change)?

2. Does your character have a problem with overindulgence in food, or drink, or some other addiction? What weakness or loss is the overindulgence trying to balance or temper?

3. Does your character love being challenged by the elements of water, fire, or both? How does he or she channel that? As a glassblower? A chef? A triathlon competitor? An environmentalist or park ranger working to ensure the health of the environment?

4. Does your character live on an island (surrounded by water) that exists because of a volcano? Is the island itself a character?

5. How is your character tested and tempered in your story?

Devil

This is another card that frequently shows up in films and television—when the reader flips over the Devil, everyone looks over their shoulders for the bad guy.

In a story, the bad guy—or antagonist—is not necessarily a person. Sometimes, the antagonist in a story is a group of people, like a mob or a family. Think Capulets and Montagues from *Romeo and Juliet*. Sometimes, the antagonist is an institution like a company or a church. An antagonist can even be a force of nature, like the shark in *Jaws* or the volcano in *Dante's Peak*. The antagonist might be the supernatural, such as the ghosts in *Ghostbusters*, or technology, like the robots and artificial intelligence in *I, Robot*.

The protagonist needs an antagonist to push against, to struggle with, and to serve as another threshold guardian in order to take the actions necessary for change.

As antagonist, the Devil raises the specter of evil, darkness, perverted power, the fallen angel, and sin. Say the word and people either shiver or cross themselves. This is also the card that misleads people into believing that the Tarot is an instrument of . . . well, the Devil! How all these dark aspects are handled in a story is determined by the genre of the story. Horror, suspense, romantic comedy, paranormal, and cozy mystery would represent the Devil and his aspects differently. Nevertheless, two qualities of the Devil could show up in any story—denial and rule-breaking.

Denial

Cue the threatening music . . . again.

In the first seasons of the British television show *Midsomer Murders*, at some point in each episode, an arm in a dark sleeve and glove moves a branch to watch another character, or picks up a knife, or commits a murder. As a viewer, you don't know who did it until the final reveal. You just see that dark, menacing arm.

That gloved hand and arm ratchets up the tension for the viewer because it is a cue that doom looms.

In many Tarot decks, on the Devil card, he looms, usually over two characters, a man and a woman who either face away from the Devil or who are sleeping. In Ciro Marchetti's *Legacy* deck, the Devil looms large over the Fool, who sits atop an hourglass turned sideways, his face turned away. Like the couple in other decks, there is a refusal, intended or unintended, to see the Devil.

Why would the Fool do this? Why would you or your characters?

Because it is easier to deny what you don't see. If you don't see it, it can't be true, it can't exist, like the toddler playing peek-a-boo who covers his eyes, believing that if he can't see you, you can't see him. Refusal to see and acknowledge what is wrong or evil is what often causes conflict, not just in a character or a story but in the world, as with Hitler.

What the character refuses to see can be highly personal or global, again, depending on the genre of the story. What finally forces them to look at something; what they do as a result is key to the conflict and its resolution.

A refusal to see can also sabotage your story during the editing process.

You are probably familiar with the statement "The Devil is in the details." It is an idiom implying that what may seem simple on the surface is more complex than it appears. This idiom is true when it comes to writing the first draft of a novel and even more so, in the editing of it. Because you can't just skim the surface of your story and then happily send it off to an agent or editor.

Some writers think one pass of editing over a first draft should be sufficient. But the Devil lurks in syntax, spelling, punctuation, passive voice, and other editing concerns. The longer and more complex your novel is, the more you need to pay attention to details. And the easier it is for the Devil to trip you up.

Like an alcoholic (or other person with an addiction), in order for change to happen, the alcoholic must first admit there is a problem, stop denying it, and then commit to taking action.

For your characters, the chains of denial could be about addictions, but also about patterns of behavior keeping a character tied to the role of victim or from moving forward with their life. The Devil is sometimes the shadow (to use a Jungian term) aspect of the character. Who wants to look into or at the shadow? Easier to pretend it isn't there. For your hero or heroine, this might be their arc for your novel, moving from denial to awareness and action.

The refusal to see the threat makes the shadow bigger than it is, but the only way to know for sure is to . . . look.

But the Devil isn't always about breaking chains of denial. Sometimes the Devil is about breaking the rules, often through humor.

Rule Breaker

Rules and structure simplify life by eliminating the need to make new choices every day. If you know you have to use Times New Roman as the font for your novel submission, for example, you don't spend time dithering about whether to use Calibri or Arial or a dozen other fonts.

The catch, though, is that the rules can become a prison (see the Tower) if you fail to push against them and even break them as the occasion demands. If writers did not break rules of writing, you would not be able to read *Ulysses* by James Joyce, or *Jamaica Inn* by Daphne Du Maurier, or *The Adventures of Huckleberry Finn* by Mark Twain, or many others.

While the shadow side of the Devil (and there is plenty of shadow) is often about addictions, temptations, evil, and so forth, there is, of course, a brighter aspect to the Devil—that of the rule breaker, mischief maker, and the stand-up comic.

In the early seventies, a black comedian, Flip Wilson, embodied this playful aspect in one of his most popular skits. His character Geraldine Jones is asked by Reverend Leroy (another of Wilson's characters) why she'd bought a third dress that week. Hand on her hip, Geraldine brazenly responds with an answer that became a national expression, "The Devil made me do it!"

In your story and with your characters, the Devil tempts with a choice—to stay within the safety of structures and rules, or to break those rules and break free. While some temptations should be ignored (like taking a second piece of chocolate), there generally is no reward for being obedient just for the sake of obedience.

So, the Devil halts you in your journey forward to make you question and reexamine those rules.

It's easy and comfortable to get used to following everyone else's rules for writing (hence the popularity of all those *How to Write* books), but those rules are made to be broken, as shown by the classics mentioned above. Like the Devil, breaking rules can be both a good and a bad thing. You don't want creative chaos. And you don't want characters breaking their personal rules just for the heck of it. Red lights hang at intersections for a reason.

But you may need to strengthen your rule-breaking muscles to give your story its chance to be the best it can be, especially as you edit and polish. Many of the most successful people in the arts and entertainment, as well as in business and in science, became successes because they broke rules.

Don't hesitate to break a few yourself and claim, like Geraldine, "The Devil made me do it."

And in breaking rules, in facing the dark, then you often have to deal with the Tarot card that comes after the Devil . . . the Tower.

The Devil's Questions for You

1. What don't you want to see about your writing or your story? Is it hard for you to give it a critical eye? Do you need to hire a good content or development editor to help you see what you can't (or won't) see?

2. Do you use a copy editor or proofreader to clean up your manuscript, or do you use a software program for that purpose?

3. Do you know and understand some of the basic rules of structure, plot, scene, and character arc? How does that help you write your story? Are you aware of when you break the rules?

4. Do you enjoy writing from the villain's point of view? Or do you have a real sense of humor that comes through in your story?

Your Character as the Devil

In fiction, the Devil shows up as himself in books like Stephen Vincent Benét's *The Devil and Daniel Webster*, Clive Barker's *The Scarlet Gospels*, and the paranormal Dark-Hunter series of Sherilyn Kenyon. He shows up in other characters who seem like evil personified, such as Jack the Ripper, and the wicked stepmother in "Snow White."

In television, he's shown up in everything from *Fantasy Island* to *Northern Exposure*, and he shows the same adaptive quality by appearing in films like *Little Nicky* (Rodney Dangerfield as Lucifer), *The Witches of Eastwick* (with Jack Nicholson), and the 1973 classic *The Exorcist*.

Whether he appears as himself or in the guise of someone else, the Devil in story is usually a source of fear, of soul-binding contracts, lust, and perverted sacrifice. He or she could be a CEO who sells the company out from under the employees, leaving them jobless, or a Wall Street stockbroker who defrauds clients.

The candidates for characters as the Devil in disguise are many. The challenge when writing this character is to avoid writing him or her as a two-dimensional cliché.

The Devil's Questions for your Character

1. Which character is not what he or she seems to be? Such as the lawyer who isn't honest, or the cop on the take, or the woman who is more manipulative than caring?

2. Is one of your characters suffering from an addiction such as alcohol, sex, or gambling?

3. Is your protagonist refusing to see something in their life, actions that bind them up in something they don't want to be part of? Who, if anyone, forces them to stop denying and to take action to free themselves? What event catapults your character into awareness and a decision to change?

4. Who in your story is the rule breaker? Do they break rules just to break rules? Do they break rules in order to be true to who they are? Or do they break rules as part of a daring, playful personality?

5. Who tries to force the rule breaker into a mold or force them to be like everyone else? What is the motivation for that character? Fear, jealousy, righteousness?

6. Is one of your characters actually the Devil? What role does that character play in the story? Motivator, rule breaker, tempter, mischief maker, a threat?

Tower

The Tower is what I call the Rock 'n' Roll card.

The Tower represents the structures in your life from which you draw your sense of self, your identity. Something earth shattering happens—parents die, jobs are lost, physical well-being is temporarily or permanently changed—and your sense of self is shaken.

When this card appears, I advise clients that it is time for them to rock 'n' roll before the Universe does it for them. You can choose to shake things up around your creative work or, sooner or later, something else will. In a novel, this shake-up of self or circumstances is often the Black Moment.

Those dark moments are a part of life, and as with life, you cannot write a novel without the dark stuff—it's called conflict, a necessary element in a novel. Conflict means the struggle or battle between two opposing forces, such as desires, goals, or people. Ultimately, the struggle reaches a crisis point, the Black Moment.

Black Moment

The novel *War and Peace* is a powerful work of historical fiction because of its juxtaposition of normal life with war in Russia, light and dark. Perhaps this is why paranormal romances have become so popular—the heroes are so very dark before they find the light of love.

In writing fiction, the Black Moment (how much darker can you get), is often the climax of a novel, the moment in which the main character realizes all may be lost. The Black Moment sets the reader up for the big emotional payoff of the happily ever after, or at least a happy for now.

Some writers, especially new writers, have a challenging time getting that Black Moment to be black enough, even in the editing process. While some writers enjoy torturing their characters with everything they can throw at them, other writers tiptoe around that dark place, because the emotional violence of it (note, I didn't say physical violence) is hard to write about. The Black Moment doesn't mean people must die, or the world has to end, or blood and gore must ensue. It does mean that your hero or heroine must reach a point in the story that feels cataclysmic, a moment in time that is emotional, mental, physical or spiritual hell. In a romance, that might be the place where the love interest has rejected or seems to have betrayed the hero or heroine. In a murder mystery, the Black Moment might occur when the detective character believes he or she will never find justice for the victim. Your character might lose a job, receive a rejection of some kind, or face a loss.

Everyone experiences Black Moments, usually more than once in life. Sadly, unlike a novel, there isn't just one Black Moment followed by a forever happily ever after. But those challenging moments of your personal life provide the power to illuminate your characters' Black Moments . . . if you are willing to go there, to shake the tower.

Depending on genre and conflict, those moments vary in intensity and what's at stake.

Your novel must have that moment. It's the peak of the conflict. And the more intense or dark the Black Moment, the more the resolution and ending of your novel will be thrown into the light, leaving your reader with so much satisfaction and contentment that you are practically guaranteed sales of your next book.

And just as the Tower is a challenge, it is also a gift, because out of that moment that shakes your characters (and you), transformation occurs.

Transformation

Whenever one of my three sons approached his midteens—you know, that time when they want to learn to drive, attend late-night parties, and start experimenting with alcohol and other things you don't want to even imagine—I wanted to build a very tall tower in our backyard and put that teenage son in it.

But no one in their right mind would do that to their kid. Right?

So how desperately protective (and possessive) was that witch feeling about Rapunzel to put her in that tower?

After all, being a girl or a woman alone is a dangerous thing. How was the witch going to leave the tower every day to do her work of gathering herbs and casting spells if she had to constantly worry about what Rapunzel, her precious "daughter," might be up to? Who knows what trouble could have befallen Rapunzel without the safety of the tower.

Funny thing is, even though Rapunzel couldn't get out into the world, the world came to her in the form of a hunky prince.

"Rapunzel, Rapunzel, let down your hair, that I may climb the golden stair."

Who wouldn't let a hunky prince in after such sweet words? Even though she'd been warned to never ever let in strangers. Remember? The world is a scary place.

In many decks, the Tower is illustrated as being struck by a bolt of lightning, which is what shakes it up and causes its destruction.

Think of it as an incident, idea, or revelation that comes from outside the supposedly secure structure of the Tower. Like a hunky prince. It is his entrance into the Tower that shakes it up and begins its destruction. The world enters the Tower, and Rapunzel's secure if narrow world is shaken and changed. Eventually, she achieves freedom. Not without loss or pain or grief, of course. Nevertheless, she and her life are transformed.

Just as Sleeping Beauty is freed from girlhood and her old life when she climbs the stairs to the forbidden tower and finds the old woman with her spinning wheel.

Whether the towers are in fairy tales, historical Europe, or today's modern cities, they provide elevated views, protection, and pride (the I'm-bigger-than-you contest). But is life lived in a tower really a life?

The shake-up and breakdown of the Tower is awful in the moment, but in the aftermath, liberation and transformation are possible.

Writers get pretty protective of their literary babies. After all, they gestate them, incubate them, give birth to them, and then help them develop.

Like Rapunzel, though, sooner or later your story has to leave the tower in order to have life in the world. And that means you and your work will be subject to criticisms, critiques, and, in the case of editors, reshaping and modifying until you almost don't recognize it.

Excuses keep the story walled up and "safe." Excuses like "I need to do another revision." Or "I don't think it's ready."

But why did the witch put Rapunzel in that tower? Was it to protect Rapunzel? No, the witch walled up Rapunzel to protect her own feelings. I wanted to put our sons in that tower to keep them safe, yes, but more so I wouldn't have to experience the emotional wear and tear and worry of those three teenage sons.

Your story can't live in a Tower. Neither can your characters. Neither can you. Eventually, there is a cry, a push, a mutiny for freedom.

The Tower's Questions for You

1. When something isn't working in your story or writing process, do you fight making changes or do you rock and roll with them?

2. When you reach that point in your story of the Black Moment, do you hesitate to go dark?

3. Do you lock up your stories in a tower (your computer tower) to keep them and you safe, to avoid moments of rejection and disappointment? Do you have a plan for dealing with rejection and writing disappointments?

4. How do you or can you transform the energies of rejection and disappointment into motivation to get back to writing and submitting?

Your Character as the Tower

Often, the role of the Tower is played by an event, the lightning bolt out of the blue that sends your protagonist and other characters reeling. Sometimes a natural disaster like the volcano in *Dante's Peak* is the lightning strike, while sometimes it is an action of violence as in *Olympus Has Fallen*. And still other times, it is something simply human, like a sudden death, a request for a divorce, or the pink slip telling your character she's lost her job.

In fiction, the Tower as a human character is someone who creates or causes all kinds of chaos, who makes people second-guess themselves and their identities. Consider a toxic parent who constantly makes a character question who they are, what they can do. The parents' goals are undermining and sabotage instead of protection.

Employers can be Towers, as can partners and spouses. The transformation aspect of the Tower could show up in a teen character, or in someone trying to recover from a Black Moment in their lives (not the story's Black Moment). Think of Harry Potter and that lightning bolt mark on his forehead. After that event, he and his life were never the same.

The Tower's Questions for Your Character

1. What cataclysmic event (in your character's mind, at least) has forced your character to make a change in their life or way of thinking at the start of your story?

2. How well does your character handle life-changing challenges?

3. What is the Black Moment of your story that forces your character to change or transform? Is it black enough?

4. Who is trying to protect or, alternatively, undermine your character without the character's knowledge or permission?

5. What is the transformation that results from the challenge or shake-up?

Notes

DOCKING, DELIVERING, AND CELEBRATING

Eventually, you arrive at your destination. You breathe a sigh of relief. You've made it! In spite of rough weather, pirates, doldrums, and even a threatened mutiny, your story ship is pulling into harbor.

You've written "The End" and you've edited and reedited. You can see the pier and folks waiting onshore to greet you. Right?

Have you ever deplaned and walked into an airport expecting to be met by a friend or family member or even a hired car, and no one was there? What happens? You make calls. You might search out other options. You wait. And wait.

Did you send a follow-up note or make a call before you left to confirm your departure and arrival?

Your lack of communication about the journey of your story and its publication can leave you waiting too. Waiting for recognition, for welcome, for sales.

This is why typing "The End" on your first draft is not the end of your journey. It's also why, several revisions further on, it is not the end of your story's journey either. Your journey with your book is not done until you've done marketing and promotion. Not just once, but repeatedly.

And because the last few cards of the Tarot's Major Arcana are all about reclaiming the light (limelight), in the following chapters you'll learn what the Star, the Moon, the Sun, Judgment, and the World have to say about launching your book.

11

Trusting Guidance and Inspiration for the Homeward Journey

For thousands of years, people have looked up at the night sky and been bewitched by the magic, mystery, and romance of the stars and the moon.

Stories of Nature's night lights were shared around the fire. Songs about them were sung to sweethearts and sleepy infants. Men used them as road signs across land and sea. Individual stars and groups of stars, constellations, were named and studied and charted. Life patterns were predicted. Among the nine Greek Muses, Urania is the Muse of astronomy, the study of the stars.

Star

The Star makes an appearance in the Tarot as guide and inspiration, and as part of something greater, offering hope and healing. And the Moon encourages dreaming, romance . . . and just a little bit of crazy.

The Star,
Tarot of the Sevenfold Mystery
by, and courtesy of, Robert M. Place.

Moon,
Retrospective Tarot,
by, and courtesy of, Ciro Marchetti.

Inspiration

After the breakdown of identity and structures experienced with the Tower, loss of hope is a normal emotional response, which is why the light of the Star is so wonderful. She illuminates the dark places enough to help you find your way out. She's the light at the end of the tunnel. However distant she might be, she still offers guidance and inspiration.

Once you start through the edits on your manuscript, it is not uncommon to doubt whether your writing, your story, has any merit at all. You might feel like the walls of your story and your identity as a writer are shaking and rumbling, threatening to come down at any moment. Is your story even salvageable?

The Star says yes. She sheds light on all the places that need polishing in the story. And she sheds light on all the places in the past where you've succeeded to do what you set out to do. Suddenly, pinpricks of light illuminate you and the story. You only need to do a scene twist here, pick up a plot thread there, and cut back on all those adverbs.

If you remember what your destination is, the goal for your story and your writing, then you can check the stars to see if you are headed in the right direction.

Sometimes the Star is a book, or a beta reader (a nonprofessional reader who reads through the manuscript for craft or story problems), or a coach, or an editor who can help you see what is wrong—or right—about your book. With the exception of the beta reader, the more experienced they are, the brighter the light they can shine on your writing.

Look to the successful writers in your genre, the Stars of your writing heritage, for inspiration. Read their books, their bios, and their interviews to discover how they work, the paths they took to success, the failures they experienced. Julia Cameron, author of *The Artist's Way*, talks about how usually all an audience sees is an artist's successes. They don't get to see the bad films, the tossed canvases, and the marked-until-unreadable manuscripts. But they exist, they are there. And seeing how the greats, the "stars," can fail yet go on to succeed acts as both guidance and inspiration.

Constellation

The star is a star merely by being itself and shining. A star does not compete with the moon.

Instead, each star shines in its own place in the universe. The Star in the Tarot encourages you to do the same, to shine where you are with your own unique light.

All those stars on the walk of fame in Hollywood didn't get there because each of those stars tried to be a Lucille Ball or a David Bowie.

They also didn't get there by themselves. Each star was part of a constellation of mentors, coaches, agents, directors, producers, and others who contributed to their success.

First, the Star inspires, then it illuminates the way for you to inspire others in turn. And in the process, you become part of a constellation.

No writer achieves success alone, not even with the ability to self-publish today. At the least, you rely on your audience and the internet. Even better, you hire a professional editor and cover designer as part of your constellation. The brighter the stars who are part of your team, the brighter you will shine.

Find other constellations and stars like yours to serve as models (but not molds) for your writing and your writing business. Like many other businesses, the publishing industry relies on connections. Your constellation may start out small, but if you attend conferences and engage on social media, your constellation will grow over time.

Just as it takes a neighborhood to raise a child, it takes a constellation to successfully launch a book and writing career. Give your story a chance to really shine.

Then, remember that your story has the power to be a star for others, to guide and inspire just as you have been.

Be the Star and shine.

The Star's Questions for You

1. Are you ready to shine, to take center stage and share your enthusiasm and excitement for your book?

2. Do you intend to finish the journey of publishing, marketing, and promoting your book alone, or to be part of a constellation of agents, editors, mentors, marketers, and others who help you shine even more brightly?

3. Who are the stars or role models that guide and inspire you as you write and pursue your writing career?

4. How will you shine and inspire others?

Your Character as the Star

Many characters in fiction look for a chance to shine or take center stage in their life. Others are more private. Think of the difference between ebullient, outgoing Tony as compared to reserved, never-take-the-spotlight Gibbs on the television show *NCIS*.

The Star might show up as a prima ballerina, or an actor, or model, or a concert pianist. It might be a character who should take center stage with a gift or talent but doesn't want to be seen or known for one reason or another, like stepping on the toes of a sibling, or because "that kind of thing isn't done" in the family.

Or the Star might be a character who was a star and now steps into the role of teacher and mentor. Think of Patrick Swayze's character in relationship to Jennifer Grey's in *Dirty Dancing*.

Even more simply, your character might be an astrologer, or astronomer, or astronaut.

Star's Questions for Your Character

1. Does your character want to be a star someday? Are they taking appropriate actions to get there or trying to take short cuts and not succeeding?

2. Who are the role models for your character? Who does your character not want to be like?

3. Does your character want to shine but has a dark secret from the past that prevents this?

4. Does your character provide inspiration or guidance for someone else? Is that a desired role or one that feels uncomfortable or undeserved?

5. Does your character prefer to shine as part of group rather than on his or her own?

Moon

Even though man walked on the moon in 1969, it somehow still retains an air of mystery and magic apparent in books, film, and television.

"La luna! La bella luna!"

This line is from the popular film *Moonstruck*, starring Cher as Loretta Castorini and Nicholas Cage as Ronny. Loretta's grandfather says it as he is out walking his several dogs on the streets of Brooklyn. He pauses to admire the bright full moon, waving his hand to move the attention of his dogs to it. Then he begins to howl and yip. Soon he and his dogs are all howling at the moon.

The movie and its title exemplify two of the strong aspects of Tarot's Moon card: lunacy and romance.

Lunacy

The root of the word "lunacy" is, of course, the Latin word for moon, "luna." *Lunaticus* was the Latin term for lunatic or moonstruck. It was believed that the full moon induced insanity and triggered certain illnesses such as epilepsy, or conditions like being a werewolf or vampire.

Along with lunacy, or as a result of lunacy, the moon is also associated with illusions, visions, and dreams.

Obviously, an active dream or visionary life doesn't indicate lunacy, but in a world that often values science over intuition and the unknown, it can be mistaken as symptomatic. Think Joan of Arc, for example, who led her army because of her belief that she heard the voice of her God. In today's world, she wouldn't be leading an army; she'd be confined to a mental institution.

According to legend and myths, the full moon is a time of transformation, e.g., shape shifting (werewolves) and other denizens of the paranormal.

And the dark of the moon, like the full moon, is also a good time for murder and mayhem. Ask any police officer. The English detective television series mentioned before, *Midsomer Murders*, often shows the full moon with the sound of a barking fox (the sly trickster) just before a murder is committed.

In *Moonstruck*, under the influence of the full moon, Loretta breaks out of her confined world to do something that seems totally senseless (or lunatic) to her, which is to fall in love.

In this phase of your writing journey, while you finish editing and revising and prepare to start promoting your story through social media, book tours, and interviews, it is easy to go a little crazy from either the chaos of it all or the expectations you and others place on you. Like the phases of the moon, this stage is temporary. Work with your constellation (team) through each phase.

In *Moonstruck*, Loretta's aunt and uncle are also caught by the spell of moonlight streaming into their bedroom and demonstrate that lunacy is not the only effect of the moon.

Romance is, too.

Romance

Maybe it's because you have to be a little crazy to fall in love in the first place, but the moon and moonlight are definitely romantic. Many romance films have a scene with the full moon shining down on the couple falling in love, who are parked overlooking a city or by a body of water illuminated by its light, or sharing a strand of spaghetti, as in *Lady and the Tramp*. A full moon signals romance.

In *Moonstruck*, Loretta's aunt and uncle experience a night of passion they thought long gone at their age, all because the moon shines in their bedroom window.

Moonlight, while bright, is not as bright as the sun. Its illumination is a little more forgiving. What would look old, wrinkled, or worn in the light of the sun merely looks softer in the light of the moon. Too, because of the shadows beyond the moonlight, a feeling of intimacy is present, increasing the romantic ambiance.

What does romance have to do with your writing journey?

Everything. You want to romance your readers. Many writers (agents and editors too) think that the goal of social media and a newsletter list is to have a high number of readers and followers. While a higher number generally offers a better chance of more sales, what really makes the difference is not numbers but engagement.

As with a couple in love, engagement means an ongoing serious relationship. Which is what you need with your readers to ensure not just sales of the first book, but sales of the second, third, and every book thereafter. Choose carefully how and where you build those relationships, because, just as with a romantic relationship, you need to be consistent about and committed to taking action, even if you'd rather be the hermit in the forest and just write your books.

The time for hiding in the shadows—or your studio—is over.

The Moon's Questions for You

1. Are you at the beginning phase of developing a following for your book? What social-media platforms are you most comfortable with? Do you have a newsletter?

2. Do you have support lined up for different phases of marketing and promoting your book? What do you need to learn? Who do you need to contact?

3. What do you love the most about your story? What passion do you have for a topic or issue in your story—like firefighting, animal rescue, or sex trafficking? How can you share that love or passion in interesting bits on social media or in your newsletter?

4. How do you love to interact with readers? Via newsletter? Social media (which platform)? Book signings? Readings?

Your Character as the Moon

Lunacy in fiction is not unusual. Heathcliff in *Wuthering Heights* immediately pops into mind. No, he wasn't a raving lunatic, but he was moody and dark and slightly on the edge.

In the light of the full moon, every werewolf and other shape-shifting creature is forced to transform, whether they like it or not, in novels by authors like Stephen King, Anne Rice, Patricia Briggs, and Kresley Cole. The conflict for that character is often one of identity or acceptance or both.

Under the light of the Moon, your character might be driven to acts of violence and anger or tempted to succumb to seduction. She might be the priestess of a local pagan circle, leading rituals on the full moon, or a lovesick swain singing—or holding up a boom box (as in *Say Anything*)—outside his beloved's bedroom window. The Moon might be the cat burglar operating in the dark phase of the moon.

Moon's Questions for Your Character

1. What secrets does your character have that they prefer not see the light of day? How does that secret affect their life? Does it affect a significant relationship?

2. Does the Moon in her phases affect one of your characters, either through mood or actions or physical form? Is there a situation that repeats cyclically?

3. Does your character prefer nighttime for work or play? Is he or she a night owl? Do dreams play a role in his or her life?

4. Is your character a romantic? Maybe too much so? Not enough?

5. Does your character's job require that they work at night? Like a night watchman, or a nurse, or doctor on night shift?

Preparing
for Delivery and
Publication

After the sweet but gentle light of the Star and the cooler white light of the Moon, you now sail your story under the bright and direct illumination of the Sun, the practical, powerful, creative Sun.

In myth, as in history, the sun has been associated with powerful figures. One of Louis XIV's sobriquets was *Roi Soleil*, Sun King. Both gods and goddesses from many different cultural mythologies, including those of Asia, Africa, North and South America, and Europe, have been associated with the Sun. In Greek mythology, of course, there is Apollo, and Japanese myths tell of the goddess Amaterasu, whose emblem, the rising sun, appears on the Japanese flag. In ancient Egypt, the earliest deities associated with the sun were goddesses like Bast, Hathor, and Sekmet.

These deities embodied power, generativity, and creativity. They also sometimes represented rebirth, as from their understanding, the sun dies or sinks into the earth, the Underworld, at night, and is reborn each morning.

Sun

With its light, the Sun brings clarity, just what you need at this point in the journey of your story—clarity for making decisions about whether to self-publish or go with a traditional publishing house, and which agents and editors to approach. You need to shine a bright light on all these decisions.

The Sun card in the Tarot helps you shine a light for clarity and to use the conscious side of your brain for making decisions, as well as providing resources you need to get your book published.

The Sun,
Legacy of the Divine Tarot
by Ciro Marchetti.
Courtesy of Llewellyn Worldwide, Ltd.

Clarity

Nothing illuminates quite like the Sun at noon, a time when shadows are almost nonexistent and everything stands in sharp relief.

Clarity is necessary at every step of your writing journey, but at this point, you need clarity about the final stages of delivering your book to readers. Whatever your dislike of the marketing, promotion, and sales aspects of being a writer, now it is time to get clear about your responsibilities to your book. Those responsibilities didn't end with "The End." In fact, much like children, your responsibility is never at an end.

If you want your book to succeed, that is.

The Sun's bright light helps you clearly see what you need to do to give your book every chance to reach readers.

With the rising of the sun, regularly, if not daily, do your part to market and promote your book. You made a plan for departure back when you wrote the first words of your manuscript. Now you need to create a plan for arrival and delivery that lays out your decisions about how to publish, what conferences to attend both for learning and for networking, and what agents and editors to query or meet with at events.

Clarity is also about allowing others to see you clearly. Remember that the Sun is a star. Its magnetic power keeps the planets in orbit around it. How will you present yourself to your readers (branding in its simplest form)? Allowing your book and yourself to be seen in a clear light is the way to attract readers. When the Sun shines, things like your writing career grow.

In addition to clarity, the sun, with its life-sustaining energy, also contributes a practical dimension: resource management.

Resource Management

The Sun is a source of life. It is also a measure of time. While the Moon's phases define the months and tides, the Sun measures both the shorter (days) and longer (seasons) cycles of life.

Time and energy and growth. Resources that the Sun bestows and that you as writer need at the end of your journey. You've moved from the internal clock of inspiration and intuition to the external clock of publication and promotion.

To meet the demands of that clock, you need to manage your resources, especially at this stage of the journey when you are tempted to think, "Oh, I've arrived. The journey is finished, and I can sit back and let others do the work."

Uh, no. Thirty years ago, before digital publishing and in a very different industry climate, you might have been able to turn the publishing tasks over to your editor and her team. That is not true today, especially if you are self-publishing or working with a small house. Many writers balk at this point, but if you manage your resources and access your constellation of support, you can do it.

First, be sure you are eating a healthful diet and getting plenty of rest. Nothing depletes the willpower to get things done like fatigue. Exercise also helps the mind operate with more clarity.

Second, make sure you schedule time to play, however you define that term, whether it is an hour on the floor with your child and Legos, a few minutes outside playing catch with your dog, or a week's vacation on the beach, catching up on your reading while you catch some rays. Play is critical to the creative mind. Think of it as another kind of food.

Third, make time for family and friends. No, not hours on Facebook or Twitter. Lunch with your hubby or wife, dinner out with your nearest and dearest, or pizza and a movie with the neighbors. Or go for a hike together.

Fourth and finally, be sure to spend time with other writers, whether it is meeting for coffee and critiques or getting together at conferences. The community of writers will keep you informed, inspired, and supported.

The sunshine of those four things will keep you growing and flourishing.

The Sun's Questions for You

1. Do you want to take on the tasks involved with self-publishing? Or do you want the support of a publishing-house team?

2. What tasks should you assign to someone else, such as editing and cover design? Do you have the budget to pay for someone to edit and design?

3. Are you willing to wait months or even a year or more for the book to be released by a traditional publisher? Will you be satisfied to have it published digitally before it is published in print?

4. How do you want to be seen by your readers? How are you consciously (or unconsciously) branding yourself?

5. How do you manage your resources of health and time? Do you get enough sleep, spend enough time with friends, etc.? What do you need to change?

Your Character as the Sun

There are some people who are just naturally sunny, outgoing sorts. In fiction, they are the hippie, the flower child, the Earth Mother, the über gardener, the happy-go-lucky guy, the summer sports figure. He is the character that brings things to light, like Ducky on *NCIS*. It might seem counterintuitive to think of a forensic pathologist as the Sun card, but in spite of his profession, Ducky is usually a happy, easygoing guy who talks to the dead and brings to light the sources of their demise.

The Sun is Mary Lenox in *The Secret Garden*, who struggles to bring life back to the garden and to her uncle and cousin. Or it's Pollyanna in the film by the same name, always thinking positively. It's the practical father figure who shines benevolently on everyone in his family, sharing his largesse. It might also be the character who is too open, innocent, or naïve.

Sun's Questions for Your Character

1. Does your character present a sunny front for everyone but has a storm brewing beneath the surface? Why the front? What is causing the storm?

2. Is your character too innocent for his or her own good? Who does that frustrate or worry? Who is happy to take advantage?

3. What character's happiness and optimism are expressed creatively? What form does it take?

4. Is your character a health and fitness fanatic? Do they carry their fanaticism too far? What happens?

5. Is your character a journalist, uncovering conspiracies and other things hidden in the shadows?

13

Announcing the Arrival: Marketing and Promotion

As you sail your writing ship into harbor, people need to know you've arrived. Word must be spread that you have goods to be sold, goods they want.

And the Judgment card embodies the role you now have to play.

From the earliest decks, the Judgment card shows at least one angel with a trumpet, sounding a call to the people below. Often, people rise out of coffins to answer the call. But, as Rachel Pollack points out in her book *Tarot Wisdom*, it's important to note that no one in the card is being judged. Rather, they are being called to celebrate, to participate in a new life or new vision.

Judgment,
Tarot of the Sevenfold Mystery
by, and courtesy of, Robert M. Place.

Judgment

An announcement has been made in the loudest possible way, not by voice but by trumpet, a sound that travels some distance. Just what needs to happen for your marketing and promotion.

Calling to Your Readers

The angel with the trumpet is reminiscent of times long ago, when news and announcements were delivered not by broadsheet or newspaper (since most people couldn't read) but by the town crier (who could). Dressed in finery, he'd take his place in the center of the town square and blow a horn or swing a handbell or cry "Oyez, oyez, oyez!" (Hear ye, hear ye, hear ye!) to get everyone's attention and command silence. Once he had their attention, he would read the news, announcement, or proclamation. His role was key to the citizenry's ability to stay informed about political and social events and concerns.

A related position or role was that of herald, usually an official of the military or government who often carried messages between leaders. Mercury (or Hermes) was the herald of the gods.

As captain of a ship that just docked with goods to sell to the general populace, you want the town crier to move among the townspeople and announce your arrival.

While traditional publishing houses still do marketing and promotion, unless you are already one of their successful top-selling authors, their budgets for marketing and promotion are not as big as they once were. The long-term book tours around the country for book signings and speaking engagements are as rare as a white tiger. Many smaller, boutique publishers ask their authors to lay out their own well-developed marketing and promotion plan that includes ideas for book signings, blog tours, social-media posts, speaking engagements, and more, usually at the author's expense. Even some of the midlevel houses expect you as the author to carry a significant portion of the responsibility of marketing your book.

If you are an introvert and protective of your privacy, this may feel uncomfortable and challenging, but, as previously stated, if you are a published author, you are also a businessperson.

You have to blow your own horn to let your readers know about your book. If you've interacted with your potential audience through social media or a newsletter, at speaking engagements, and in other ways, they want to know the book is finally available. By now, they are eager to buy it, read it, and spread the word about it to their friends.

Don't be shy about it. If you had just delivered a baby, you would be excited to share the news, and your friends and family would be happy to hear about it.

You have delivered a baby—your book. And marketing and promotion is your way of sharing the exciting news of that birth. Think of it in those terms and you won't feel so uncomfortable about the sales aspect of being a writer.

Book signings, giveaways, contests, and book reviews are ways to share your excitement.

To put out the call to your readers.

The Call to You

Just as you have to sound your horn to attract readers to your books, you also have to answer the call of other horns.

This card, in some decks, is called "Awakening." While you have completed one book journey and called others to share in the excitement of its arrival, you are probably hearing a call yourself, a call to awaken to new opportunities, purpose, and vision.

First, there are the literal calls (or emails or texts), from bloggers, event organizers, and media who want to interview you or invite you to speak. If the idea of doing any of these things makes your hands tremble on the keyboard, then look at the three figures usually found on the Judgment card. They are the key to making yourself comfortable with interviews.

It's a trick I learned years ago when I published my first book, *Weaving a Woman's Life*. Decide on three things that you want to be sure to communicate about yourself and your book, no matter what direction the interviews take. Choose three scenes, or a character, a scene, and a special element of the book that you can talk about with enthusiasm.

Use the number 3 to set criteria for whose calls you'll answer. You don't necessarily want to do every interview or reading or event. You want to be sure (1) that the source of the call has a good reputation, (2) that the venue reaches your audience, and (3) that the event or interview serves your vision and purpose for your book and writing career.

These interviews are important because your reader or your potential reader wants to purchase a piece of you right along with the book. This is why, in addition to the book blurb on the back cover, there are a few sentences about the author and an even more detailed bio inside the book. The reader wants to know who you are.

The readers you call to and the calls you answer are key to your book's success.

And, ultimately, your writing journey's success.

Judgment's Questions for You

1. You are not the same as you were before you started writing the story. What is different in your perceptions of yourself as a writer/author?

2. What are you willing to do to issue the call to your readers? What is easiest for you to do? What feels like a stretch? Will answering that call make the biggest difference in the success of your book?

3. Can you get someone to help you prepare for it? Like a speaking coach or someone to do a practice interview with you?

4. What are three important things you'd like your readers/audience to know about this book and your journey with it?

5. Who among your friends and connections would enjoy helping you get the word out?

6. What new story ideas are already brewing and calling to you?

Your Character as Judgment

In myth, Judgment appears as the phoenix, reborn and transformed, and, of course, as angels. It is the Egyptian god Osiris who was the judge of the dead and represented life after death. It is Persephone who descends to the Underworld for half of the year and then returns to life for the other half.

It's both Beauty and the Beast, for Beast issues the call and when Beauty answers, they are both reborn, she in her independence from her family, and he to his human self.

In fiction, vampires and zombies represent the darker aspects of Judgment, of rebirth, as do angels in many paranormal novels like those by Nalini Singh.

Judgment's Questions for Your Character

1. Does your character experience a rebirth of some sort—emotional, physical, mental, spiritual? Does that rebirth come at the beginning or end of your book? How does it affect others around him or her?

2. What call has your character heard? A call to service such as in the military, or in a nonprofit service organization like Doctors without Borders or Greenpeace?

3. In answering the call, is your character so idealistic that the practicalities of life escape them or are beyond them? Do they have someone who takes care of the practical things for them? How does answering the call affect the relationship?

4. Is this character a recruiter of some sort? Do they recruit because they believe in the cause or because it is just another source of income? Or because it makes them feel special?

5. What new creative vision, inspiration, or idea calls to a character? Do they answer? Why or why not? What happens if they answer? If they don't?

14

On Top of the World

Hey, you've arrived! Your ship has safely docked.

Oh, the relief to be able to set foot on solid ground again! After weeks and months (and sometimes years) of worrying if you'd ever make it to the end of the journey. Much like delivering a baby, the relief is accompanied by fatigue and a sense of floating in time and space. And if anyone asked you at the moment if you'd have another child (i.e., write another book), you'd probably hit them over the head with your manuscript.

World

You're on top of the World, right now, and it's time to acknowledge your work and achievement and to celebrate.

Celebration

The World card conveys a sense of triumph and success. The Fool, who took a risky leap to start the journey through the Major Arcana with the Magician, has finally arrived at the end of the journey, the World. And here the Fool stands, arms outstretched, as if to embrace the wholeness of self, fully revealed. The struggle to achieve, to prove oneself worthy as storyteller, as a creative person is at an end.

The World,
Legacy of the Divine Tarot
by Ciro Marchetti.
Courtesy of Llewellyn Worldwide, Ltd.

For now . . .

It's important to not let the opportunity for celebration and acknowledgment of your achievement slip by.

Celebrate with those who helped and supported you along the way. Acknowledge them as you acknowledge your efforts. Some acknowledgments will show up in the front or back matter of your book, of course, but it is also wonderful to send personal notes to some of the key stars in your constellation. And don't forget to acknowledge and thank your readers and audience. A little appreciation can go a long way.

Celebrate and bask in the rewards. The celebration might be a special dinner with a loved one, a shared bottle of champagne, or a big party. Whatever your choice, really enjoy it, savor each moment, each accolade. You deserve it.

Because tomorrow . . .

Preparation

Whether tomorrow is the day after your book's release or several weeks after, tomorrow you prepare for a new journey.

Yes, you've achieved a pinnacle and are on top of the World. It may be your first time here or your tenth or one hundredth time, but you know there is always another story to tell. Maybe the next in a series, or maybe a new theme, or a new genre or a new character who whispered in your head while you worked to finish and edit the last book.

Before you begin again, just as the ship's crew cleans the ship, repairs her sails, and scrapes barnacles from her hull, you need to prepare for the next journey. Preparation might be cleaning up your office or studio. Preparation might also include time away from writing to refill your creative well (Temperance appreciates that). It also might include a plotting retreat with other writer friends where you brainstorm book ideas and plotlines.

Time away to let the writing muscles rest and relax, gathering energy for the next book, is important. Time away with family and friends breaks the isolation that can set in. Indulge in opportunities to laugh and play (the Sun).

Then brave up to take the next leap, because the Fool's journey is always beginning again. Just like the circles on the World card—sometimes the world or a wreath or the zodiac—the life of a writer and the journey of the Fool never end.

You come to the end, only to begin again.

The World's Questions for You

1. What are you feeling at the end of the journey with your book?

2. What have you learned from the journey about yourself as a writer and about writing in general?

3. Whom do you want to celebrate with? Whom do you want to thank or acknowledge? In the book? In other ways?

4. What length of time do you need as a break before beginning on the next book? What can you do during the break to help you refill your creative well?

5. Do you need to change anything about your work space or writing tools to make writing and editing, marketing, and promoting easier for you?

Your Character as the World

This character can be anyone who has reached some level of achievement, like an Olympic athlete receiving a gold medal. The achievement can be anything from a championship to a graduation, a promotion, or the awarding of a grant or exhibition.

The World card signifies reaching a pinnacle, but for most people in most circumstances, that pinnacle is only the first of many. It may seem like a president or a queen or the owner or CEO of a large company has no other pinnacle to reach, at least in that arena, but that doesn't mean they sit back and do nothing for the rest of their lives. Exploring the next pinnacle, what journey is worth taking for someone already at a pinnacle, is a story worth writing.

In fiction, the World could be Sherlock Holmes, who is the smartest and best at solving crime. The World could be any superhero with superpowers. What journey takes them to new places, new levels of development and growth?

The World is also an elder, someone who has lived a long and happy life with a successful career and relationships. What is their journey? Perhaps with grandchildren or through participating in a cause, lending wisdom and insight, or having to adapt to new technologies or new ways of doing things. Or through resolving a challenge or situation from the past, like Helen Mirren's character in *Woman of Gold*, who takes on the Austrian government to recover a Gustav Klimt painting of her aunt that was stolen by the Nazis.

The time spent on top of the World is often brief. What happens after the Happily Ever After? Often, it is where the character chooses to go from there that makes for an interesting story.

The World's Questions for Your Character

1. What pinnacle has your character reached? Is it age, career, reputation, sports, love? How did they get there? What are the consequences and how will they show up in your story?

2. Has your character failed to reach a pinnacle and, therefore, is punished for it in one way or another? What led to the failure? Will your character try again or try for a different pinnacle?

3. Does your character lack motivation of any kind? Do they want to constantly celebrate with friends, spend money, and have a good time? How will this affect relationships? How does it catch up with them?

4. Is your character someone who is always helping others achieve their dreams, reaching their pinnacles but never going for his or her own? Like a parent living out his or her dreams through their children? What prevents your character from striving to achieve something for themselves?

5. Is your character an elder, someone who has wisdom, knowledge, or experience to share with others? Are they doing that? Why or why not? If not, who or what gets in the way? Do they have the energy or commitment to move past any obstacle?

Notes

PUTTING IT TOGETHER

15

Four Elements for Storytelling

Just as a ship's journey is influenced by the four elements of earth, air, fire, and, of course, water, so are the journeys of your book and story characters.

As mentioned in chapter 1, these classical four elements are represented in the Tarot's four suits of the Minor Arcana (small secrets), which appear much like the four suits of modern playing cards. In readings for your writing, they offer more detailed information about personality traits, settings, important props, and even secrets and plot twists.

Suits of the Minor Arcana

Remember, the four suits and their associated qualities are the following:

Wands (Fire): spirit, creativity arising out of passion and will, career, work, inner drive

Cups (Water): heart, emotions, love, relationships, dreams, intuition, creativity that arises out of longing and love

Coins (Earth): body, home, health, wealth, the five senses, the material realm, creativity manifested

Swords (Air): mind, thoughts, attitudes, beliefs, communication such as writing, teaching, creative inspiration

As you can see, all four elements play a role in the creative process because creativity and writing engage the entire being. Nevertheless, when I do readings for book-coaching clients, I often see cards from the suit of Swords turn up in number, reminding me of the adage "The pen is mightier than the sword."

Don't worry about your knowledge of the cards. Whatever deck you are using, you can easily use the cards to answer questions about your writing just by looking at the images on the cards and noting details such as colors, objects, and figures and their positions.

You can use these details to create a believable world for your story whether you are writing contemporary or historical, mystery or sci-fi, or literary or genre fiction. Your reader wants the experience of stepping out of their "real" world into your land of make-believe and to experience it as if they were one of your characters.

The Senses

To put your reader in the scene, some writing books stress the importance of using the five senses—smell, taste, hear, see, touch. Other books and teachers advise using a few senses well.

When you walk into a room or out your front door, you aren't immediately aware of your environment with all five senses. Sight is usually your primary sense, followed by other senses. Which sense your character perceives his or her environment with along with sight will not only help you set the scene but also reveal something about your character. For example, a gardener might step out the door and smell the loamy scent of wet earth, while a musician might hear bird's song. Someone chased by a bad guy is more apt to have their ears peeled for footsteps than noticing the sunset (unless they have to find an escape before dark). Which brings to mind two of my favorite movies that reveal the importance of the senses.

In *Wait until Dark*, Audrey Hepburn plays a blind woman, Susy, who has become the unwitting recipient of a doll containing drugs. When the bad guy finally figures out who has the doll, he comes hunting. In a scene labeled one of Bravo's *100 Scariest Movie Moments*, Susy fights for her life in her apartment, where she has broken or unplugged all the light fixtures to put her enemy in the dark with her. The movie is very much about the sense of sight but also, as you can imagine, the sense of hearing.

In *Like Water for Chocolate*, the heroine, Tita, loves to bake. She also loves Pedro, but as the youngest daughter, in the tradition of her family, she is not allowed to marry and must stay single to care for her mother. As the story unfolds, whenever Tita bakes something, the emotions she is experiencing as she bakes emerge in her food and affect others when they eat it. In the film—and the book—taste becomes a primary sense, as does touch.

Details, like the senses, are important in creating scene and in world building. The details you leave out can be as important as the details you include. And more is not necessarily better.

In the time of Victorian writers like Charles Dickens and Jane Austen, descriptive passages were extensive, and were used to set mood. Remember Miss Havisham's table with its ancient wedding breakfast and cake in *Great Expectations*? But modern readers don't have the patience of the Victorians. To keep your readers' attention while also putting them into the world of the story, be selective about your details.

And this is where the Tarot is helpful, especially with the pip cards (1–10) of the four suits of the Minor Arcana.

First, you can pull several cards—I like the number 3—and then look at the images. See what sensory details immediately catch your attention. A full sail on the 6 of Swords? Then maybe a soft breeze, or a warm draft from a fire might be useful in your scene. A garden in blossom on the 9 of Coins? Maybe a unique scent will add dimension to your scene, attracting or warning a character.

Or, you can think of sensory details in relation to the suits—Coins for touch, Swords for the sense of hearing (think sound waves, air waves) and smell, Cups for taste, and Fire for seeing. Or assign the suits to whichever sense seems logical to you. Remember, the cards are a tool and you can make up your own rules on how to use it for your writing. Lightning will not strike you if do something outside traditional Tarot thought (which even Tarot experts can't agree on).

Or, assign a number, one to five, to each of the senses, and then shuffle the first five cards of the four suits (so 20 cards), then pull two or three to see what to focus on in your current scene.

But why do this at all? Surely, you can figure this out on your own?

Sometimes you can. But sometimes you are so focused on what you think should happen that you forget about other possibilities. One tweak or one twist on a scene can make all the difference. I worked with a client on a critical scene in her story. She thought she had the setting (by the ocean) and the sensory details clear, but when we pulled a card there was the full moon. The author realized that the scene needed the light of that moon to reflect on the water, setting the mood for a spell her heroine casts. Although obvious after we pulled the card, she had so much going on in her mind about the scene, she didn't see it.

Pulling cards for sensory detail and other elements in a scene will sometimes confirm what you already were writing or had in mind. And often, it will give you more to think about, opening you to other possibilities.

The same is true for settings.

Location, Location, Location

Have you ever bought a house? Rented an apartment?

If so, then you know the location of your residence is important. Some people like to live in a large city, others prefer suburbs, and still others, like me, the country. Some people want to live where it is warm all year, while others like a change of season. Others want to be near water, or in the mountains, or near family or far away from them.

Sometimes the choice of where to live is determined by a job or by relationships, but if you have the ability to make some choices about your home, then you've chosen to live in a place that suits you.

Your story needs a home that suits it as well.

And just as your home is in a location that is part of a larger location or community, your story has a "neighborhood" too, a neighborhood of all the novel's settings. Even if you are writing a story about a master spy who travels to Berlin and then to Bali and finally to New York City, that is still the story's neighborhood.

Sometimes, though, the location isn't just the story's home, location, or setting; it is also a character. Think of *The Revenant*, starring Leonardo DiCaprio. Winter in the unsettled west of the United States in the early 1800s is the antagonist that DiCaprio is forced to conquer in order to survive.

But setting doesn't have to be a life-threatening, natural phenomenon like a fire or a tsunami to be a character. Any iconic, legendary, or mythic setting can act as character in your story. In his book *The Breakout Novelist*, Donald Maas asks, "What does the setting of your current novel mean to the characters in it?" A character who grew up in the country and hates everything about tall buildings, large crowds, and continuous noise is likely to have an antagonistic relationship with New York City.

Pulling a few cards from your Tarot deck will help you create a personality for your setting by focusing on setting details, making your location three-dimensional instead of just a two-dimensional backdrop.

Pull a few cards and use any or all of the imagery, the meaning, and the numbers, to see what captures your attention or provides new ideas or information about your settings. A 4 of Coins with a figure holding tightly to coins might suggest a bank, or the Securities Exchange Commission, or a pirate hideaway, depending on your story and genre. The 5 of Wands might be a jousting field, a boxing ring, or an art auction. Additional cards could give you more detail about the setting, such as rustic, elevated, or near water.

Pull a card for each of the locations you have in mind and see what each card says to you about its related location, as well as looking at how each card relates to the others and what that reveals to you and adds to your story.

Or, do one of the character spreads for your primary setting.

Remember to use only what moves your story forward and anchors your reader in your world. Anything else is just grist for another mill.

Props

If you've ever traveled by train, plane, or ship, then you know that space is at a premium. Squeezed into the small space of an airplane's bathroom are all the same items that you'll find in the roomiest of powder rooms—toilet, toilet tissue, sink, soap, trash bin, and mirror.

Keep that efficiency and good design in mind as you think about the props you'll use in your story. Do not get carried away describing that lovely Victorian settee upholstered in brocade fabric embroidered with long-tailed birds. Unless . . .

Unless a frantic neighbor rushes into your protagonist's house with her baby and lays the baby on the settee, and the baby spits up (or worse). Now that lovely settee is stained. How the neighbor reacts and, more importantly, how your protagonist reacts can reveal a lot about the traits of your characters. If that settee recurs throughout the story because your protagonist loves (or hates) it and things happen around it, then that prop is used efficiently in the design of your story. It counts.

A prop can reveal aspects of a character like the deerstalker hat in Sherlock Holmes (the hat is worn by deer hunters and thus shows Holmes's hunting character), signal a change in mood or scene, like an appearance of a pet as in many of Kristan Higgins novels, or become a powerful symbol, such as the ring in *Lord of the Rings*.

When you are in the heat of your first draft, you may not pay much attention to your props and whether or not they belong. But when you begin on edits for your story, be aware of the props that pop up repeatedly. Pull some cards and see if the objects in your scenes belong, and if they do, how they are earning their keep.

If you are uncertain about how the pip cards relate to props, look at objects in the scene of the card. Also, think about what the element of the suit might suggest in terms of shape or function. For instance, a Coin could represent a coin in your story, but it might also represent anything else circular like a wheel, ball, watch, or clock face. A Cup might represent a cup, but it could also be a pot or other vessel, a pool, or an urn holding ashes or flowers. A Sword could be a pen, as mentioned, a cattle prod, an acupuncture needle, or a hat pin. Wands could be a shepherd's crook, an arrow, a signpost, or a conductor's baton. Be willing to let your mind play with what shows up.

The possibilities are endless, especially if you play with more than one deck.

Especially if you play with spreads.

16

Spreads (Maps) for the Journey

A spread is the intentional layout or placement of cards in a Tarot reading. Each position in the spread has a meaning to it. For instance, the three-card spread for Indiana Jones represented his past, present, and future. Each card was looked at in relation to its position in the spread.

Almost every Little White Book (LWB) or larger book that accompanies a Tarot deck offers at least a couple of spreads that you can use with the deck. In addition to that, within Tarot literature there are dozens if not hundreds of books on Tarot spreads on any topic you can imagine.

What is offered here are a few spreads specifically related to writing fiction. You can use these as shown or add to them with questions from the previous chapters. Also remember that any of the questions in the previous chapters can be used individually as a spread or together with the other questions of that section as a spread.

Significator/Character

In readings done for clients with questions unrelated to writing a book, the Tarot reader will often include as the first card in the spread a significator. The significator is usually the card that represents the person being read for or the theme of the reading.

For your purposes, the significator can represent the theme of your book or scene, a character that you are asking about, or yourself in relation to your writing. You choose whether to draw the card randomly after shuffling and cutting, or choose it deliberately because it seems to appropriately represent you, the theme, or the character you are reading for.

For instance, your protagonist is the CEO of a company. This person sees the big picture, knows where they want the company to go, and takes action. You deliberately pull the Emperor card because here is a take-charge kind of person. Next, you formulate your question. Structuring the question, being clear about what you want to know, is an important part of doing a reading. The clearer and more precise your question, the clearer you will be about the answers the cards give you.

You want to know what this character's biggest need or want is outside of the business, because there has to be something more going on with a three-dimensional character than just a drive to succeed.

Before you pull cards, jot down your questions. Put them in an order that makes sense to you. Focus on one question, like what is the character's biggest need, or use as many questions as you like. A caution here. If you are new to using Tarot, I suggest keeping a spread to ten cards (or questions) or less.

Back to your Emperor character. If you ask what his or her biggest need is outside of the business and what keeps the character from getting that need met, lay out two cards, one for each part of the question.

Using Ciro Marchetti's *Tarot Grand Luxe*, I pulled the Emperor card, then shuffled and drew a card for the biggest need and a card for what blocks his need. Here are the three cards.

The Emperor,
Tarot Grand Luxe
by Ciro Marchetti.
Courtesy of US Games, Inc.

Three of Wands,
Tarot Grand Luxe
by Ciro Marchetti.
Courtesy of US Games, Inc.

The Magician,
Tarot Grand Luxe
by Ciro Marchetti.
Courtesy of US Games, Inc.

The Tarot always delights me with what it reveals. The story posed here just by these three cards is intriguing and full of potential.

Card 1, the Emperor, is all about external power. If you remember from the chapter on the Emperor, his two words are authority and structure. Certainly, in Marchetti's image of the Emperor, there is authority in his posture and structure all around him.

When I turned over the card for what this Emperor needs, I grinned. The 3 of Wands. Pretend you know nothing about the Tarot. Just look at the picture. Imagine that is the Emperor standing on the shore. What does he need? What immediately came to mind when I turned over the card is that the Emperor is longing for adventure, or an opportunity to get away from his responsibilities and the strictures and structures that surround him. Maybe he just needs a vacation or maybe he is tired of being in this position of leadership.

Now look at what blocks this need—the Magician. His two words are attention and focus. So, the Magician could represent the antagonist who is using tricks to keep the Emperor focused on the wrong thing, which creates all kinds of problems. He could be a wise advisor who thinks the Emperor should keep his mind on his responsibilities and has no problem reminding him of them when the Emperor starts talking about taking a break or getting away. Or the Magician could be another aspect of the Emperor who keeps telling him to keep his focus on what's important.

Even if you do not know the traditional meaning of the cards or the two words associated with them in this book, you could simply look at the pictures and get ideas for your story and possible answers to your questions. Reversing the second and third cards would give you other ideas and possibilities, but here is where you use your High Priestess power of trust and intuition. How do the images and ideas resonate with you and your story? If they don't feel right or don't get you excited about story ideas, pull more cards around one or both of the cards or reshuffle and pull two new cards. They are a tool for you to use.

What if you want more insight into this Magician character and his (or her) role in your story?

Then lay out more cards beneath the Magician card. You could just pull three cards to see what turns up, or you could ask specific questions as with the Emperor and pull a card for each question.

If your Emperor character is a minor or secondary character in your story, then these cards give you a wealth of ideas to work with. However, if he or she is a primary character, then you'll want to pull cards for other questions, like "What pushed this character into the Emperor role?" and more. You don't have to pull cards for the character all in one reading either. As your story unfolds, more questions will arise, so pull more cards.

Plot Spreads

There are hundreds of books about how to plot your novel. Plotting is a challenge for writers, especially those working on their first books. Hence, the reason for all the books. And the two different camps of plotters and pantsers.

The challenge for plotters is losing the excitement for the story at some point in the manuscript because everything is known. For pantsers, the challenge is getting happily to the middle of the story and then bogging down with uncertainty about what should happen next.

Both camps can use the Tarot to get themselves out of the tight spots.

The most obvious way to pull cards for your plot is to choose your plot structure, like the hero's journey or Michael Hague's seven-point, five-act structure or James Scott Bell's Mirror Moment Golden Triangle. Once you've chosen the structure to work with, pull cards for each point or aspect of the structure. If one plot point card isn't clear enough, pull a few more cards (1–3) to place beneath that point and see if that helps. Remember, the story is yours and the plot structure and the cards are tools to help you, not restrict or limit you.

If nothing gets your story engine going, then maybe it's time a for a walk or a conversation with a friend. Then come back ready to play again. Yes, play. The Muse loves to play with you, whether writing your story or pulling Tarot cards.

The Unseen

The Unseen? What am I talking about?

After all, before you turn over the cards, it's all unseen. Still, I often find it helpful when I do a reading for a client—or myself—to pull the card at the bottom of the deck to represent what I am not aware of: the Unseen.

Even as you shuffle and turn over cards to answer your story questions, you have in mind ideas and answers that *should* show up. For instance, when I pulled those two cards for the Emperor character, I expected to see the 2 of Cups show up to indicate his need for relationship with a significant other. I did not expect to get the 3 of Wands. Because I wasn't attached to the outcome or results of the reading, I was delighted to see the Wands card.

But if I was attached to the results and expecting the 2 of Cups, I might not like that Wands card. The Unseen card is helpful because it brings to light something you aren't paying attention to. Remember the Magician's focus and attention? Often, you can be so focused on what you think should be happening in your story that you fail to give attention to other possibilities. The Unseen card says, "Hey, you are forgetting to pay attention to this. This could be important. Think about it."

The Unseen card makes you the Hanging Man, turning you and your perceptions about your story upside down. It's also the Devil, suggesting you break rules and get playful.

Try a one-card reading for any aspect of your writing or story, asking, "What am I not seeing? Whether you use one card or all 78 cards in a spread for your book, how you structure the spread is up to you.

And now, to end this book, I pull a card to represent the last word from the Tarot. It is the Lady (or Page) of Coins. Here she sits with the Coin in her lap. Coins represents the physical realm, and to me the Coin is the book, the idea made physical in a way that helps you create beauty (the rose) in the world with your stories. It is also the Tarot card or deck that helps you make that book real.

Lady of Coins,
Tarot of the Sevenfold Mystery
by, and courtesy of, Robert M. Place.

Lady of Wands,
Tarot of the Sevenfold Mystery
by, and courtesy of, Robert M. Place.

Then, for the Unseen, I turn the deck over and discover another Lady/Page, the Lady of Wands. According to Robert Place's little white book that accompanies this deck, this Lady "represents a change of circumstances, claiming new territory as one's home, comfort overcoming uncertainty."

I hope this book does that—helps you claim new territory in your writing, changes how you feel about the process, and dispels uncertainty as you work to tell the story you were meant to tell.

The Tarot is both map and compass, helping you to find your way across an ocean of words and ideas to a story that, on completion of the journey, makes you as happy as it will make your readers.

Be brave. Take a leap. The journey is one well worth taking.

Bon voyage!

Notes

Resources for the Journey

Resources listed below are ones taking up shelf or digital space in my personal library of books and decks. I've read them, used them, and value them. Remember, they are resources, not rules. Some of them have exercises, questions, and structures for plot or scenes you can use for creating your own spreads for your writing.

Books on Writing

Alderson, Martha, and Jordan Rosenfeld. *Writing Deep Scenes: Plotting Your Story through Action, Emotion and Theme*. Cincinnati, OH: Writer's Digest Books, 2015.

Bell, James Scott. *Write Your Novel from the Middle: A New Approach for Plotters, Pantsers and Everyone in Between*. Woodland Hills, CA: Compendium, 2014.

Coyne, Shawn. *The Story Grid: What Good Editors Know*. New York: Black Irish Entertainment, 2015.

Cron, Lisa. *Wired for Story: The Writer's Guide to Using Brain Science to Hook Readers from the Very First Sentence*. Berkeley, CA: Ten Speed, 2012.

Cron, Lisa. *Story Genius: How to Use Brain Science to Go Beyond Outlining and Write a Riveting Novel*. Berkeley, CA: Ten Speed, 2016.

Dixon, Debra. *Goal, Motivation & Conflict: The Building Blocks of Good Fiction*. Memphis, TN: Gryphon Books for Writers, 1996.

James, Steven. *Story Trumps Structure: How to Write Unforgettable Fiction by Breaking the Rules*. Cincinnati, OH: Writer's Digest Books, 2014.

King, Stephen. *On Writing: A Memoir of the Craft*. New York: Scribner, 2000.

Lukeman, Noah. *The First Five Pages: A Writer's Guide to Staying Out of the Rejection Pile*. New York: Fireside Books, 2000.

Maass, Donald. *The Fire in Fiction: Passion, Purpose & Techniques to Make Your Novel Great*. Cincinnati, OH: Writer's Digest Books, 2009.

Maass, Donald. *The Breakout Novelist: How to Craft Novels That Stand Out and Sell*. Cincinnati, OH: Writer's Digest Books, 2010.

Maass, Donald. *The Emotional Craft of Fiction: How to Write the Story beneath the Surface*. Cincinnati, OH: Writer's Digest Books, 2016.

Pressfield, Steven. *The War of Art: Break Through the Blocks and Win Your Inner Creative Battles*. New York: Grand Central, 2002.

Vandermeer, Jeff. *Wonderbook: The Illustrated Guide to Creating Imaginative Fiction*. New York: Abrams Image, 2013.

Vogler, Christopher. *The Writer's Journey: Mythic Structure for Writers*. 3rd ed. Studio City, CA: Michael Wiese Productions, 2007.

Weiland, K. M. *Outlining Your Novel: Map Your Way to Success*. Scottsbluff, NE: PenForASword, 2011.

Software for Writing

Autocrit: www.autocrit.com. Manuscript editing software for fiction writers.

Masterwriter: www.masterwriter.com. Language tools and reference dictionaries.

Scrivener: www.literatureandlatte.com. Word processing, outlining, research.

Websites for Fiction Writers

Helping Authors Become Writers: www.helpingwritersbecomeauthors.com. Author K. M. Weiland's site offers hundreds of articles on writing fiction. Her About page has the links to her podcast and other goodies.

Holly's Writing Classes: www.hollyswritingclasses.com. Holly Lisle is an expert at writing fiction and offers many online courses. She's written for traditional publishers and has self-published. Her site offers community, instruction, and support.

Writing Organizations

International Women's Writing Guild: www.iwwg.org. International community of women writers of fiction and nonfiction. Annual conference, online interviews, classes, and more.

Mystery Writers of America: https://mysterywriters.org. Newsletter, contests, mentorships, and other benefits for members.

Romance Writers of America: www.rwa.org. National and international chapters and members, online courses, print magazine, and more.

Science Fiction and Fantasy Writers of America: www.sfwa.org. Support, promotion, and information.

Books on Tarot

Dean, Liz. *The Ultimate Guide to Tarot Spreads: Reveal the Answer to Every Question about Work, Home, Fortune and Love*. Beverly, MA: Quarto, 2016.

Place, Robert M. *The Fool's Journey: The History, Art & Symbolism of the Tarot*. Saugerties, NY: Talarius, 2010.

Pollack, Rachel. *Complete Illustrated Guide to Tarot: How to Unlock the Secrets of the Tarot*. London: Elements, 2002.

Pollack, Rachel. *Tarot Wisdom: Spiritual Teachings and Deeper Meanings*. Woodbury, MN: Llewellyn, 2008.

Tarot Websites

Aeclectic: www.aeclectic.net. A useful site for seeing the varieties of themes and styles of hundreds of decks.

Amazon: www.amazon.com. Along with everything else under the sun, this site also lists at least 1,000 Tarot decks (some of which are not Tarot but oracle decks).

eBay: www.ebay.com. If you search by using "Tarot deck," you're likely to get thousands of listings that include old and new decks, in English and other languages, at a variety of prices from a few dollars to hundreds of dollars. Some are real collectibles; some aren't. Do your research before buying.

The Tarot Garden: www.Tarotgarden.com. A good resource for a variety of decks both used and new.

Favorite Tarot Decks and Creators

Dean, Liz, and Craig Cross. *The Game of Thrones Tarot*. San Francisco: Chronicle Books, 2018.

Marchetti, Ciro. *Legacy of the Divine Tarot*. Woodbury, MN: Llewellyn, 2009.

Marchetti, Ciro. *Tarot Grand Luxe*. Stamford, CT: US Games Systems, 2019.

Place, Robert M. *Tarot of the Sevenfold Mystery*. Saugerties, NY: Hermes, 2012.

Radiant Rider-Waite Tarot. Stamford, CT: US Games Systems, 2003.

Ryan, Mark, and John Matthews. *The Wildwood Tarot: Wherein Wisdom Resides*. New York: Sterling Ethos, 2011.

Quick Reference Guide

This quick reference guide is just that—a guide. Remember to trust your intuition and first responses to the cards in relation to your writing and story. You will see possibilities that aren't mentioned here. This is just a reminder and a starting point so that you can let your mind and Muse play.

The Major Arcana

Fool: The leap into the unknown; risk, instinct, innocence

In Writing: Take a risk, begin, the condition or mindset of every hero and heroine. Children, an innocent; a lover of risk and its thrills, the guy who doesn't want to be tied down, the wanderer.

Magician: Moves idea into form, knows how to keep and use focus and attention, is confident in his or her performance

In Writing: Keep your focus and attention on your story; believe in yourself. Often a secondary character who aids the protagonist or faces a test that transforms and gives new powers and abilities, or an antagonist, manipulator, scam artist, actual magician, wizard, or sorcerer.

High Priestess: Connection to the unconscious and deep wisdom, reveals wisdom, teaches trust in intuition

In Writing: Invites you to trust your intuition and your story, to go deeper. Threshold guardian who tests the protagonist's deepest fears; the spinster reluctant to move out of her virginal world; nun, advisor to primary characters, the wise crone, the witch or fairy godmother; insists she knows what's best for everyone; controls others through the secrets she knows.

Empress: Ultimate mother, nurturer, abundant creative source, goddess of love, sexuality; fertile and fecund

In Writing: Emotions of your story, abundant creativity, the need to nurture self or story or both, time to create from the heart. Queen, protective or overbearing mother, person seeking love through sex; hippie or girl next door, one who loves animals or being outdoors; a gardener.

Emperor: Ultimate father, figure of authority, leadership, structure, establishes and upholds the rules

In Writing: Helps with big picture of your story, to plan and structure to your story, to keep you on deadline. King, CEO, or micromanager; strong leader or petty tyrant; a commanding officer or political leader; uses power for good or ill.

Hierophant: Source of knowledge and tradition (especially spiritual), celebrant, ritualist, mentor, supports the Emperor in upholding laws and structure of society

In Writing: Traditions of writing, discipline, time for a mentor. Priest, ascetic, missionary, guru or disciple, leader of a cause, librarian, mentor, professor, religious revolutionary, cynic or skeptic.

Lovers: Union with the divine, ecstasy, choice, decision, love, commitment, loyalty, friendship, collaborator, business partner

In Writing: Love of your story, or warns against giving it too much at the expense of other relationships. Hero and heroine of a romance; someone in love with a career, a cause, a business rather than a person; someone obsessed with someone; young lovers, a love triangle.

Chariot: Speed, victory, success, progress through diligence, overcoming adversity, pulled in two different directions, travel, carelessness, accidents, running roughshod over others

In Writing: Create momentum with your writing, set goals, mark progress. Someone driven to succeed regardless of the cost; feels they have no control over their life; fought the odds and succeeded; a race-car driver, jockey, jet pilot, runner, a winner or champion.

Strength: Fortitude, inner strength, confidence, courage, will, endurance, creativity, animal passions, obstinate, weak, at the mercies of one's desires

In Writing: Easy control of your story, keep confident, care for physical needs, balance hard work with rest and renewal. Character exhibiting strength and endurance such as a well-trained athlete or soldier; someone who works their way back from a challenge; who leads safaris or outdoor adventures; wildlife photographer, zoologist, veterinarian, libertine, or gourmand.

Hermit: Solitude, silence, seeker, solitary, guiding light, sage, old man

In Writing: A need for quiet, solitude, or time away, especially to hear your Muse; time to seek out a mentor. Teacher, nature guide, mountain climber, loner, private eye, college professor who likes his ivory tower; the withdrawn paranoid, wise sage.

Wheel of Fortune: Fate, fortune, shift of fortunes, destiny, bad luck, a failed enterprise

In Writing: Steer your story, determine its time of development; a turning point in your story, seeing patterns, a setback. A gambler (especially on the roulette wheel), a spinner, the captain of a ship, a time traveler, an investor, someone who has the power to affect others' fates.

Justice: Balance, harmony, fair play, truth, integrity, honest self-examination, dishonest, bigoted

In Writing: Balance between structure and imagination; willing to tell the truth of your story; time to examine creative habits, or to edit; awareness when signing contracts. A judge, a lawyer, an accountant balancing books, a police person, a criminal, someone outside the law.

Hanging Man: New perspectives, surrender, sacrifice, traitor, shaman, initiate

In Writing: Hung up, suspended to achieve new insights and ideas; a time to practice patience with process, agents, editors. The scapegoat, the hypochondriac, the traitor, the character in a coma or suspended animation, the yoga teacher or yogi, someone hanged on the gallows, someone in an elevated position like an arborist, or men working on the girders of a skyscraper.

Death: Endings, letting go, change leading to new beginnings, fear, a refusal to let go

In Writing: Fear of failure, fear of success, fear of putting your story out for others to read it, time to release old writing habits or work that is going nowhere. An event that brings death to a person, an organization or group, a culture or world; a person, mythic or villainous, who brings death; a fixer, someone in charge of firing during a merger, a divorce lawyer; a protagonist dealing with grief and loss.

Temperance: Interaction between inner and outer life, bringing harmony to two or more opposing elements, strengthening through testing, creativity, restraint

In Writing: Creativity, the balance between story structure and emotion, love and lust, passion and restraint, the need to strengthen the story. The musician; the artist; a glassblower or iron worker; a chef; someone who is intemperate with food, drugs, or alcohol; a drug counselor or rehabilitator; someone with a short temper; someone patient.

Devil: Addictive habits, bonds, perverted power, rule breaker, mischief maker

In Writing: Test rules, play more with your work, stop denying fears and face the darkness of your story. The antagonist, someone who likes to control others for selfish or nefarious reasons, someone who likes stirring up trouble, a "fallen angel," a prankster.

The Tower: Transformation, shake-up, breakdown, identity crisis, seeking to place blame

In Writing: A shake-up or breakdown of your identity as a writer, a crisis that interrupts your writing and requires reevaluation. The Black Moment of the story that creates transformation, that shakes up protagonist's world; event like an earthquake or other natural disaster; a toxic character who knocks others off their feet through criticism or other forms of sabotage, the overprotective person like the helicopter mom.

The Star: Inspiration, guiding light, healing, hope

In Writing: Successful authors who inspire and light the way, books that guide and inspire, the members of your publishing team. An actor, model, political leader, CEO, athlete, astronomer, astronaut, astrologer; person who likes the limelight or who inspires others.

The Moon: Lunacy, illusions, idealism, romance, dreams, intuition

In Writing: Attention to dreams while writing, daydream, follow creative intuition, allow the unconscious to play. A symbol for things revealed by its light or hidden in its shadows; call to the wild as with shape shifters, the romantic moment, dreams or nightmares; the dreamer, the romantic, someone moody, emotional; one who has a hard time with reality; cat burglar, or night-shift worker.

The Sun: Energy, growth, clarity, exposure, vitality, magnetism

In Writing: Managing resources of time and health, planning marketing and promotion, branding. Flower child, Earth Mother, gardener, summer sports figure, one who brings things to light such as the investigator, the X-ray technician, the lighting director, the investigative journalist, the scientist.

Judgment: Awakening, arising, vision, mission, rebirth, a failure to respond

In Writing: Calling to readers through online and offline means; answering the call from agents, editors, bloggers, and others; willing to share a part of self and process. Born-again religious, vampires, zombies, angels; recruiters such as for the armed services or businesses; those who have been called to serve in some way.

The World: Completion, achievement, celebration, reward

In Writing: Launching book, celebrating, continued promotion, preparing for next book, acknowledging achievement. An elder, someone at pinnacle of career or life; the Olympic champion; winner of a political campaign; the end of the story, the Happily Ever After.

The Minor Arcana

Swords

Ace of Swords: A new idea; beginning a new book, chapter, or scene. A character who is a writer, a teacher, a speaker, or other communicator; an acupuncturist; someone assertive.

2 of Swords: A choice or decision to make about your writing, needing to trust intuition, procrastination. A character pushing for a decision, someone indecisive or who makes decisions by procrastinating, a mediator, a divorce lawyer.

3 of Swords: Rejection, a harsh review, a breakup with agent or editor. A character who is grieving, heartbroken, depressed, having heart problems; a psychiatrist or psychotherapist, advice columnist, or media host.

4 of Swords: Rest, retreat, meditation, recovery. A character who teaches or practices meditation, a contemplative. A retreat center or veteran's hospital or hermitage.

5 of Swords: Battle, defeat, conflict, argument. A soldier, someone constantly in conflict with others, someone who enjoys a battle of wits and who has to be right, a bully, someone who has their priorities wrong.

6 of Swords: Escape, travel, exploring new places and new possibilities. An immigrant, a refugee, a pilgrim, a pilot or flight attendant, a foreign correspondent, a cruise ship, airplane.

7 of Swords: Sabotage, theft, fraud, legal problems. A saboteur, a propagandist, a thief, someone who threatens another's sanity.

8 of Swords: Confinement, restriction, debilitation by one's own thoughts, initiation. A character who plays the victim or refuses to take responsibility, an initiate. A mental institution, a secret organization that requires initiation.

9 of Swords: Bad dreams and nightmares, anxiety, insomnia, paranoia. A character who is paranoid, an active dreamer, an intuitive or psychic, someone anxious and stressed, someone going through menopause.

10 of Swords: Severe criticism, verbal attack, feeling immobilized by shock or disaster. A character who practices acupuncture or undergoes acupuncture, someone suffering from nerve damage or disability, someone unconscious or in a coma, stabbed to death.

Page of Swords: Smart (sometimes too smart), doesn't know how and when to curb thoughts and words, observant, sees things others miss, good problem solver.

Knight of Swords: Takes action either under orders or after thinking things through, sometimes late or misses out because spent too much time dithering. Rights wrongs. Loves argument for argument's sake. Good lawyer.

Queen of Swords: Takes no flack, sees through lies, has clear boundaries, knows the ability of words to cut both ways. Hates lies, always searching for truth and justice because strives for fairness for those she is responsible for.

King of Swords: Confident, intelligent to the point of brilliance, often makes others feel inferior as a result. Skilled communicator. A leader in fields like politics, law, medicine. Ideas are often cutting edge.

Wands

Ace of Wands: A new project with passion and push behind it, an inspired idea, a new adventure. A character who is energetic, passionate, creative; someone great at generating ideas but not necessarily following through. A short-distance runner, a branding consultant.

2 of Wands: Two creative opportunities to choose between or that feed into each other, a creative partnership, a fiery romance. A character who loves to collaborate creatively, inspired by passion and sexuality.

3 of Wands: Decide whether to wait for opportunity to find you or for you to get out there and make it happen, travel. A character who loves adventure and travel, especially to foreign lands with warm or tropical climates, for whom opportunity and success is just over the horizon.

4 of Wands: Creative stability, commitment, a new home for your work. A character ready to make a commitment to creativity, in a relationship, to a job or career; a couple getting married or going on a honeymoon.

5 of Wands: Creative competition, testing, entering contests, strong opinions, a challenge with establishing creative priorities. A character who loves competition—athletic, artistic or creative, someone in advertising or marketing, an arts critic, movie reviewer, et al.

6 of Wands: Success, victory worthy of a confetti parade, recognition, and applause. A character who's reached a point of success, recognition, applause, and accolades, a time of a big announcement, could be the high in the story before the low or the Black Moment.

7 of Wands: Stepping into the limelight or into a higher position, defending your position or that of others, tests and challenges. A character who defends others like a defense attorney or an advocate of some kind, someone whose career is in peril and has to defend it, someone who claims the right to recognition and reward.

8 of Wands: Creative flow, fast-moving energy, elements in motion and nearing completion, or stalling and creative blocks. A character who moves quickly from one project to the next, leaving others to do finishing and tying up of loose ends; a computer whiz, an accomplished and focused artist or creative, a dancer.

9 of Wands: Strength through challenges, needing boundaries even now, time to stop pushing. A character about to deliver a child or creative project, feeling the fatigue after a long labor; someone who acquiesces to everyone's demands while denying their own needs.

10 of Wands: Overwhelm, exhaustion, overburdened, doing too much. A character who martyrs themselves, bites off more than they can chew, or refuses to admit that they are overwhelmed by their own actions while refusing to ask for help; someone who is strengthened and has grown by meeting extreme challenges.

Page of Wands: Welcome news about creative projects, time to share your excitement and enthusiasm for your work. A character with a fiery nature, eager, ambitious, impulsive, creative.

Knight of Wands: Adventurous, time to explore, broaden horizons, frustration if projects don't meet your deadlines. A character who loves charging off on the next adventure, leaps before looking, restless, finds it hard to settle down, enters into relationships fast and furious and passionate.

Queen of Wands: Passion, intuition, self-expression, confidence. A character who is comfortable and confident in her sexuality, knows her own power, helps others own theirs, influential, creative, can also be jealous and angry if her own creativity is frustrated.

King of Wands: Assertive, confident, arrogance, highly creative. As a character, rules in order to wander, wants to be out conquering new territories. His energy motivates and inspires others.

Cups

Ace of Cups: The Grail, the quest for fulfillment of the heart's desire, a new mission or vision, new love. A character falling in love for the first time, or encountering a new passion or project, finding a true purpose, or newly pregnant.

2 of Cups: Partnership, relationship, romantic relationship, collaboration, reconciliation. A character in love, the couple in a romance novel, close partners in a business or marriage, family counselor, a matchmaker or dating site.

3 of Cups: Deep emotions, close connection to friends, celebration, a strain on relationships, creativity in projects. A character who values relationships with friends. A series of novels based on a group of friends. Any close-knit group like a military unit or a sewing circle or members of Alcoholics Anonymous where relationships are close, supportive. A bride and her wedding party. A coffee shop or local eatery.

4 of Cups: Boredom, apathy, daydreaming, emotionally shut down. A character who has been wounded in a relationship and shuts themselves off from emotions; someone whose job requires them, for their own safety and stability, to shut down emotionally. A sterile work environment.

5 of Cups: Instead of shutting down emotionally, frozen by fears of future emotional hurts, loss, sadness, avoiding critical reviews of work by avoiding putting it out there. A character who is emotionally crippled, might need professional help; someone grieving a relationship loss, an "angsty" teenager, someone who plays "poor me."

6 of Cups: Nostalgia, happy memories, tapping into the inner child, playtime. A character who works with children, an antique dealer, a children's book author or photographer, an artist or writer who keeps the inner creative child alive.

7 of Cups: Distraction, loss of focus, shiny-bright-object syndrome, numerous options. As a character has a problem staying on task, staying committed to a project or a relationship, has a grass-is-always-greener attitude, or might be very imaginative, which can be good or bad depending on how they handle it, or could be a Renaissance person, talented in many areas. A battered women's shelter.

8 of Cups: Letting go of what no longer satisfies, giving up, heading in new directions before reaching completion on current projects. A character who goes with the flow, seeks new purpose or vision or meaning, or new love, is a bartender.

9 of Cups: Wish fulfilled, generosity, coming together of friends or opportunities. A character who runs a mission or a foundation, a wine maker, a mother giving birth, an adoption.

10 of Cups: Home sweet home, family bonds, social gatherings, a new home. A character who just bought a new house, a realtor, a family moving into a new home, a decorator, a caterer, the hero/ine returned home safely.

Page of Cups: Big dreams, illusions, moody, "angsty," young at heart. A character young at heart, has big dreams but a problem with keeping feet on the ground; a young artist; someone gullible, easily taken in by someone who seems to be "the one."

Knight of Cups: Wants intimacy but can't quite commit, visionary, romantic, driven by the quest. As a character could be the knight in shining armor—until it's time to commit, a real romantic with all the romantic gestures, the introvert wearing armor to protect the heart.

Queen of Cups: Nurturing, compassionate, creative, healing. As a character, a super mother, generous hearted and protective; a good listener, offers friends a shoulder to cry on, might be an intuitive, a doctor or nurse, a relationship coach or a psychotherapist.

King of Cups: Emotionally in control, responsible, success in the arts. As a character, a father who is or isn't emotionally available to his children; carries the worries of the world, has suppressed his own creativity and dreams in responsibility to others; the director of a hospital or some other healing institution, a police commissioner.

Coins

Ace of Coins: The seed of an idea for a book or project, beginning of a new venture with financial rewards, new health, new home. A character with health and vitality, the beginnings of recovery from a physical challenge, a physical therapist. A small animal, seeds.

2 of Coins: Decisions about money, home, health; working to keep money demands balanced, a need to keep track of the budget at home or work. As a character, a juggler, an accountant for a business, a financial advisor; someone keeping two sets of books, committing fraud.

3 of Coins: Creative work, crafting, exhibiting, focused work in the studio or office. As a character, an artist, writer, composer, architect, contractor; someone who presents talks or workshops. A studio or workshop, a monastery where monks illustrate manuscripts, a building under construction, a plant nursery.

4 of Coins: Financial stability, security, organization, foundation for the future. As a character, a banker, an investor, a property manager, confined to a wheelchair. The foundation of a building, a foundation or trust fund.

5 of Coins: Poverty, ill health, desperate need, fears of loss, looking for aid in the wrong places. A character with a "poor me" mindset, someone who won't ask for help, or someone who has a serious health challenge, suffering as a result of others' actions. As place, a hospital, church, an aid foundation.

6 of Coins: Generosity, a balance between giving and receiving, a loan. A character who is generous or stingy; someone who does good works but may do so for selfish reasons, a loan shark. Charities.

7 of Coins: Nearing harvest, keep an eye on the prize, potential for success, satisfaction with hard work. As a character, a farmer keeping an eye on his burgeoning crops, a hard worker watching savings grow, someone whose health is improving, a parent watching their children grow. An orchard, vineyard, farm, ranch, or spa.

8 of Coins: Journeyman, professional, devoting oneself to study or work for best results. As a character, a graduate student, a researcher, a geologist, a tour guide, someone failing to advance any further, always researching and studying but never graduating. A library, a college or university, a research center.

9 of Coins: Achievement, blooming, completion of a project, a garden or home you've designed. As a character, someone with the financial ability to travel or acquire some of the luxuries of life as a reward for hard work; someone with an innate sense of design, an eye for beauty. A walled garden, an art gallery, a museum, a restoration.

10 of Coins: Abundance, happy home, love, property. A financially secure family or couple, a wealthy man, the squire or noble of the community, a country village, a family reunion, a jewelry store or crystal shop.

Page of Coins: A child or young person happy in nature, collects coins and rocks. Has an innate connection with animals and birds, a kind of Dr. Doolittle. This Page is usually of good health. Shows a fascination with the world around them.

Knight of Coins: Cautious, grounded, a champion of Earth and Nature, a lover of beauty in all its forms, a bodyguard or policeman. Serves and protects in practical ways. Keeps his uniform and accoutrements in top shape. Would rather till the earth than ride off on adventures, a homebody.

Queen of Coins: Like the Empress, a mother deeply attached to and passionate about her offspring, whether children or the elements and creatures of the natural world. Someone who loves life, knows how to appreciate and celebrate it, is perfectly happy alone in nature, has a sensate connection to the world; a cook or chef or gourmet, a physical trainer, a perfumier, a jewelry designer, an herbalist.

King of Coins: A person generous with material goods, a CFO, successful investor, a master builder, a good boss, a benefactor. He or she shares the wealth rather than hoards it. Or he could be someone who doesn't share because always worried about financial security.

Paula Chaffee Scardamalia uses myth and fairy tale, Tarot, and dreams for her fiction and nonfiction, as well as for helping her book-coaching clients. Since 1999, Paula's taught writers at regional and national conferences, like RWA and the International Women's Writing Guild, how to write stories from the deepest part of their imaginations. She is the award-winning author of the nonfiction book *Weaving a Woman's Life: Spiritual Lessons from the Loom*, and the former dream consultant for *PEOPLE Country Magazine*. Paula also publishes a newsletter on writing, creativity, Tarot, and dreams.